It's Nobody's Business But Yours

A comprehensive guide for the woman who wants to turn her business idea into a reality

by
Barbara Killmeyer

Printed in Victoria, BC, Canada.

ISBN: 978-1-4269-2186-5 (sc)
ISBN: 978-1-4269-2187-2 (hc)

Library of Congress Control Number: 2009941118

Our mission is to efficiently provide the world's finest, most comprehensive book publishing service, enabling every author to experience success. To find out how to publish your book, your way, and have it available worldwide, visit us online at www.trafford.com

Trafford rev. 1/12/10

 www.trafford.com

North America & international
toll-free: 1 888 232 4444 (USA & Canada)
phone: 250 383 6864 ♦ fax: 812 355 4082

Foreword

Throughout my working life I have been employed by others and I have had businesses of my own. My experience prior to entering the world of entrepreneurship had been in retail sales and as a secretary and administrative assistant. For many years I worked in an office where I was responsible for all aspects of office management including a payroll for over one hundred employees. This position gave me valuable business experience which I put to good use when starting my own business.

Through my association with organizations comprised of business women I was asked to speak and this led to my first venture, *Advantages Plus*. Through *Advantages Plus* I spoke to organizations and business conventions about issues such as professional image, effective delegation, and telephone etiquette. These seminars were well received and I was asked to write articles on the topics about which I spoke. This led to my second business as a freelance writer and ghostwriter.

My years of experience with women in business has brought to my attention the problems these enterprising women faced, both starting a business and later while operating their company. I noted also their willingness to share what they have learned and to help each other avoid costly mistakes.

It has been my goal through my speaking and through my writing to provide information which will answer some questions and eliminate some anxiety for those who choose to become members of the business world.

This is the reason behind It's *Nobody's Business but Yours*. It is my hope that by reading this book you will be encouraged to see your ideas and your dreams become a successful reality.

Acknowledgements

I would like to thank my husband Donald for his years of continued support. He is my best friend and my biggest cheerleader.

I thank all the wonderful people who have contributed their experiences and advice to make this book possible.

Thank you to mentors and friends who, over the years, have given me help, taught me the correct way to do things, and encouraged me to follow my dreams.

I acknowledge the large part played by the various organizations that have provided me with opportunities to develop my self-confidence and knowledge through my association with them. These organizations include: Professional Secretaries International (currently International Association of Office Professionals), Women's Business Network, and Association of Business and Professional Women.

Chapter One

It's All in Your Head

Each business begins in one of several ways: an idea, a need, or a hobby that grew out of bounds. Suddenly the hobbyist finds that she is a businesswoman, the need has been satisfied, or the idea has taken root and grown into a full-blown plan.

Studies have shown that women who decide to strike out on their own are intuitive thinkers. They are willing to step away from the ordinary and ask "what if...?" They are tuned in to their subconscious mind and trust the messages received from it.

You may deny that you are intuitive, but how often have you accomplished something that others thought would not be possible, and when asked why you made certain decisions your answer was, "something just told me to do it that way?" That "something" was your intuition at work. If you stop to think about the number of times that you chose a particular path "just because" you will see that your *are* intuitive. It would be wise for you to tap into that power and develop it for daily use. One way to do this is by a process known as Centering. Practiced each day, Centering can open the mind to countless possibilities and help you to choose the best one for you. To use Centering effectively, sit in a relaxed position, in a quiet comfortable place for five minutes. If the passing of time bothers you, set a timer and forget about it. While in this relaxed place rid your mind of all clutter. If you are having a particular problem, focus only on that problem. Sit quietly and pay attention to the thoughts that flick through your mind. After the first five minutes are up, sit for another five minutes and think about the ideas that popped into your head. Many solutions to problems have been solved in that manner. It may take some time to learn how to clear your mind and make it receptive, but soon this will become quite easy and you will look forward to your ten minutes each day.

Everything that we take for granted today began because someone had the courage to look beyond the ordinary and see the extraordinary. They saw a need, had an idea and the foresight to pursue that idea.

Go back to the caveman and something as basic as fire. Suppose that it suddenly dawned on Urg that each time he banged a certain two stones together this hot little thing jumped out from between them. He was thinking hard about this one day when he did it around some dry grass. The next thing poor Urg knew, he had started a fire near his cave. Well, being the enterprising young man that he was, it wasn't too long before Urg had his fellow cavemen over for a cookout and he became the neighborhood hero. All right, so I made that up, but someone had to realize that fire could be harnessed and used for good.

Imagine what a different world we would be living in today if people such as Elias Howe had given up when he saw the need for a way to sew mechanically. Or suppose Eli Whitney left his idea of a better and faster way to harvest cotton die, or if Thomas Edison with his outlandish ideas concerning electricity had listened to those who said he would never succeed. These wonderful, inventive people followed their dreams and as a result we have better lives today.

Ideas and Dreams

Ideas are born of dreams. Ideas are free; they do not come with a price tag attached. Ideas are not reserved only for those who have a certain amount of education. What counts, what makes the difference, is what you do with your ideas.

Suppose, as you were growing up, each time you expressed a thought you were laughed at, or told that you were being silly and even stupid to consider such a thing. What do you think would happen over a period of time? Of course, you would begin to believe this negative input that you receive, and if you conclude that your ideas are indeed worthless, then why even pursue them?

What a tragedy! So many wonderful concepts would die before they had a chance to be born. An idea needs to be nurtured to see it come to life. True, not every notion will be a prizewinner, but how will you know which are and which are not if you don't give them all a chance?

Never allow anyone to tell you that your dreams are worthless.

However, and this is a big however, your dreams *will* be worthless, impossible, and of no value whatsoever if you just let them lie there. They absolutely must be followed by ongoing action. Beware of over planning. Does this scenario sound familiar? You get an idea that you feel will be the best thing to ever hit the public. You can't imagine why no one has ever thought of it before. You are extremely excited by the prospect of bringing your inspiration to everyone. But wait! Before you actually put your baby out into that big, wide world everything has to be perfect. So you plan and organize on and on and on until paralysis sets in and you can't get it off the ground.

Don't let this happen to you. Prepare in the best way that you can and then put your message out there. Remember that once your plan is launched it isn't the end. You can continue to plan and organize. There are constant revisions and improvements that will need to be made. These can be accomplished over a period of time.

The best possible thing you can do for your business idea is to act on it.

Filling the Need

There are women who did not have a burning desire to have a business of their own, but nevertheless found themselves in charge of a lucrative venture. Often these are women who discover that they can fill a need by doing something they love.

One such woman is Patty Kreamer, owner and president of TimeFinders, Inc. Her firm specializes in productivity and efficiency solutions. Patty is an organizer, a professional speaker and a consultant. Her career grew out of a love of organizing. She said,

"From the time I was a child I was always putting things in order, organizing everything and getting rid of clutter." She began to help relatives and friends with paper and time management and saw a growing need for her services. Now, not only individuals, but also major companies rely on TimeFinders, Inc. to assist them in finding solutions to their problems of inefficiency or low productivity. Patty recognized a need and knew how to fill it.

Patty is also a perfect example of being flexible and realizing that your initial project may not necessarily be your final product/service. Her original idea was to present seminars on time and paper management. She said, "At that time I couldn't even speak in public! Through networking the idea of individual consulting was born and my business just took off from there."

Another example of filling a need is demonstrated by Anna Marie Gire of Hot Flash Media Inc. a publishing business. Anna Marie explained, "The idea for Women's Independent Press (WIP) was conceived during a conversation with a friend who was planning to relocate to another city. Considering how difficult it is to find friends or activities in a new place, I thought how convenient it would be to have a printed guide available that listed clubs, resources, and activities to help people get acclimated to a new location."

"I pondered this idea for about a year, and then I mentioned it to a colleague, who embraced the idea enthusiastically. Then we got serious. After several months of planning and endless cups of coffee, what began as a small resource guide blossomed into a 24 page newsmagazine dedicated to women and their vast and varied interests. We named our company Hot Flash Media and our new publication Women's Independent Press. WIP was launched in March of 2003, Women's History Month."

"The original idea has transformed into an on-line newspaper, filled with the same high quality of writing and subject material as appeared in the printed version of WIP. In addition, there is a Women's Yellow Pages (WYP) in Pittsburgh that evolved from the original newspaper, which unfortunately had to cease publishing in April of 2005. WYP provides comprehensive information on a variety of subjects, as well as a directory of mostly women owned businesses."

Patty and Anna Marie are two excellent examples of seeing a need and filling that need.

Learn to think "need". When you see a product think about how it could be improved, what would make it easier to use? I'm sure there have been many times when you had to improvise with items you already had in the house to rig up a temporary solution to a problem. What if you took your rigged up solution and worked on it to make a product for marketing? Do enough people have a need for it? Would it be too costly for the average person? Would you be able to keep up with supply and demand?

Finding a need and filling that need will be an exciting challenge and could start you on the road to becoming an entrepreneur.

Hobbies Can Grow

When my friend, Mary Sweet, retired from her secretarial job she began to make cookies from a special recipe and she gave these treats to friends and relatives as gifts. It wasn't long before she was asked to make them for special occasions such as office parties, and bridal or baby showers. The holidays brought on a rush of orders and Mary had to think about just how much time she wanted to spend on this. She decided that she had other things she wanted to do during her retirement and she didn't want to be tied down to a business. Mary still makes her cookies for friends and relatives, and she will occasionally make them for a special affair, but she does not make the cookies as a business venture. Mary said, "When it stopped being fun, then I didn't want to do it anymore."

Mary made a wise decision. When you develop a hobby you do it because you enjoy the time spent and the finished product. It can be very easy to get caught up in the excitement of people wanting your product or service and you can envision booming sales and a huge profit. But there are some things you fail to consider when you're caught up in the momentum. Can you meet the demand? If you have to work ten times as much to meet the demand will you still enjoy it? Can you continue on your own or will you have to hire help? There are many more questions you can ask yourself, but the bottom line is, will I still like doing this or will it become a chore?

I am definitely not trying to discourage anyone from turning her hobby into a business. I think it's a wonderful way to go and I encourage you to give it a chance. But, I also want to be realistic and I wouldn't want you to enter a business with high hopes only to find disappointment after a time.

If you decide that this is the way for you then you are fortunate because you have a ready consumer base that likes your product and will almost certainly pass the word on to others.

Be careful when pricing, make sure to take supplies, time, and any overhead you might have into consideration. Of course you want to make a profit, but you don't want to price yourself right out of the market either. It takes a lot of serious thought to get the price just right so you can profit and the consumer is happy.

Tired of Working for Others?

Often the incentive to go into business for yourself begins with the disillusionment of working in corporate institutions. Women in particular are held down and not given the opportunity to develop talents and skills that are important in the business world. They face issues such as the glass ceiling, lower pay, and harassment.

In speaking with businesswomen I heard such comments as this one from Shirley Ledford, who operates two businesses; she sells health and nutrition products as well as another product, Fire Breakers, to extinguish small fires in the home. Shirley said, "I lost my job and I was tired of being treated like I had no "smarts". I felt I had something to offer so I went out on my own and I've never been sorry."

Shirley is not alone in her reasons. Terry Muffi has been an individual beauty consultant for Mary Kay Cosmetics for the past ten years. Terry said, "I was tired of the environment of Corporate America; the unfairness, the politics, and the glass ceiling. I was also tired of sitting at a desk all day long." Now Terry is happily helping her clients to feel better about their appearance, and she feels better about herself too, because she is making a difference in the lives of others.

Both of these successful ladies found that by leaving a job where they worked for others and transferring their knowledge to their own businesses they became much happier individuals.

The Fear Factor

Making the change from employee to business owner is not always easy. It can be a very frightening experience. After all, you are moving from a regular paycheck to highly irregular pay, from a set amount of money each month to not knowing if you will have a lean month or a good one. Once you get underway and build up a customer base and a demand for your product or service some of the anxiety will ease, but that probably won't happen for awhile. It would be best to have a nestegg that will cover you for the first few months. Will you need start-up money? We will cover that in another chapter because that is also a consideration.

The joy of seeing your plan take shape and become a reality is one of the most worthwhile and rewarding experiences you will ever have. It is worth every effort you must expend to make it work.

Patty Kreamer said it very well when she stated, "If you have a burning in your belly, a passion for your work, and plain old guts, you can do anything you want to do."

Summary

The focus for chapter one has been on the reasons a woman would decide to go into business. These included the following:

- Ideas are wonderful and can provide you with excitement and motivation. But unless you take action and do something with your ideas they will be worthless. Don't try to get everything perfect before actually getting your product or service to the market. Changes and improvements can always be made as you move along.

- Learn to develop your powers of intuition and trust in the messages you receive from your subconscious to help you to solve problems as they occur.

- At times the best plan for a business is to fill a need that is lacking. By learning to think "need" and by using your creative abilities, you can provide a product or service that will benefit consumers and grant you the opportunity to own a profitable business.

- A hobby can be the easiest and best way to expand into a business since you know your product or service is well received and you are starting out with a consumer base. Be aware though of the difference needed in expenditure, man-hours and effort before starting a business that will lose its appeal for you in a short time.

- Working for others can be a frustrating experience. For some, the way to get out from under the thumb of Corporate America is to start out on their own and work for themselves. That way they can have more control over their day-to-day work and also for their future.

- Moving from employee to entrepreneur can be frightening. There are many unknown factors, not the least of which is money. But with proper preparation all fears can be overcome and the joy of being a businesswoman overrides the fears.

Chapter Two

Scouting the Market

Everyone hopes to discover a product or service that is like no other; one that will catch the attention of the public. Obviously, this isn't going to happen if you enter a field that is already saturated. However, if you can make what you provide unique, give it a different angle, and make it special and different, then you can garner your share of the consumer dollar. This is why it is so important to scout the market and be aware right from the beginning of who your competition is and exactly what it is that they are offering.

Proper preparation is vital to the success of any venture and this includes discovering all you can about those with whom you will be competing for business. The buying public has only a limited amount of money to spend in any specific area. You need to see that you are offering something that will make them want to spend that limited money for your product or service.

Organizing the Hunt

In order to check out the competition you have to know where to find it. Don't be in a hurry to get through this, take your time and do a thorough job. Here are several places where you can find out what you are up against.

- The Internet: The Internet is one of the best and most useful tools we have today. Make full use of the advantages it gives you. A computer and Internet access is common in most homes today, but if you don't have a home computer there are places where you can still access the information. The most common is a public library. You are permitted to use their equipment, you only have to sign in and you can have an e-mail account of your own. This will make all Internet information available to you. The only drawback is that you are limited in the time you can spend at the computer. Because there are usually several people who want to use it, most libraries restrict you to a one-hour time frame. However, I have never heard of a library asking you to leave when your time was up if there was no one waiting to use the equipment. So, if the library is your option the best thing would be to find out what time is the least busy and arrange to be there at that time to have a better chance of extended use. When using the Internet go to the "search" option and enter your field of interest. A list of possibly hundreds of sites will come up on the screen. You can narrow these down to those in your geographic area. This will give you an idea of how many others are in the same business. Take time to visit each site and you will learn all you need to know such as, where they're located, exactly what services they offer, what the product does, what the cost is and much more. This is all valuable information for you. Take notes for future reference and make special note of any that are similar to what you plan to do.

- Yellow Pages: Take the advice of the telephone company and "let your fingers do the walking." Sit down with your notebook, telephone, and directory and go down the list. How many are in your field of interest? Is it small enough that you feel there would be room for you, or would you just melt into the crowd? Are there any special offers that surprise you? If you have any questions about the service or product call and ask about them. Become as familiar and as comfortable as you can with the topic.

- Newspaper Ads: Become an avid reader of newspaper classified ads. How many offer the same product or service that you will offer? How would you rate the ads, as attention-getting, well-written, snappy, or dull and boring? Clip the ads that appeal to you and add them to your notebook along with your comments about them. These will come in handy when you are preparing your own ads.

- Trade Organizations: Is there an organization in your area that focuses primarily on the type of business you are interested in? If so, join and learn from those already there. Example: If your idea is to start a secretarial service, or a staffing service for offices, then you would be wise to join an organization such as the International Association of Office Professionals. This would give you a good perspective of what is already in place, what is needed, what problems are cropping up, and what latest technology you need to know about.

- Craft Shows and Shops: If you are thinking of turning your hobby into a business, check out craft shows and stores that specialize in selling handcrafted products. You can get a good idea of what is available and what competitive prices are. If you want to sell hand crocheted tea cozies for $10 each, make sure that the customer can't get the same thing at a craft show for $5. Check the quality and variety of choices. Will you be able to offer a better product that would justify the difference in price? If not, it's time to rethink your plan.

- Word of Mouth: Remember the greatest avenue of information – word of mouth! Don't be afraid to ask friends and neighbors questions such as: Do you know of anyone in the area that takes care of pets while the owners are away? Where are they located? Have you used them? Did you like the service? Would you go to them again? Why, or why not? By asking questions you'll know what you're up against and what you need to do differently.

Find Your Own Niche Market

Finding the proper niche market for your product or service can be the difference between operating a so-so business or one that continues to grow and bring in profits.

Think carefully about your target market. How would you define it? If your answer stops at a general group, such as stay-at-home moms, people looking for a different kind of gift, or computer operators, you're missing the boat. What you are doing is defining people who *can* use your business as opposed to people who are *likely* to do so.

When thinking of your business think of individuals who all share the same specialized interests and needs. They must have a high interest in what you have to offer, and on your part, you must be able to give them a reason to deal with you rather than with your competitors. They should be easily accessible to you and finally, the size of the group is an important factor. They should be large enough to generate the amount of business you need and small enough to be overlooked by others in your field. That is a niche.

Why is a niche market important? It is important because it will allow you to tailor your sales strategy and be extremely specific in your ads. Advertising is expensive and you need to make sure you get the most for your dollar. It is a known fact that people will be less likely to respond to a general ad directed to "housewives", or "Mothers" than to a more specific ad to "working mothers with small children", or even, "single parents". By gearing your ad to your niche market you will get the attention you hoped for by the market you have targeted.

You have other advantages when you define a niche market; the greater part of your competition is eliminated, large businesses usually won't bother with it and it is easily overlooked by other small businesses.

How do you find your personal niche market? If you are already in business and have a list of customers, examine that list and try to discover a thread that is common to each of them. You might find, for instance, that most are teachers who work with exceptional children. In that case, rather than trying to sell to all teachers, you can target your advertising to those who work with exceptional children, since it is these teachers that will be most interested in your product.

Another method is to list all the benefits of your service, then make a list of individuals for whom your service would be the most advantageous. This list should give you a good perspective of who your niche market would include.

Paying attention to, and developing a niche market can help you to focus on the area that will provide you with the most sales and will also keep you from wasting time, effort, and money on ads that will not result in sales.

Evaluating the Competition

It is impossible to discover a business that has no competition. I don't know if you would even want to have such a vocation because if no one else is selling your product or service, it might be because there is no call for it.

There is no getting away from it – competition is a fact of business life, so you might as well use it to your advantage. Study it carefully to see what you can learn. What are they doing that seems to be working well? What do you see that is not so good? Most importantly, how can you improve on their product or service in your own business?

If a product is involved, purchase one, then ask family and friends what they feel is needed to make it better. You can also ask them, "what if…" and in that way you will get feedback on your own ideas. You can do the same with a service; take it on a trial basis and use the information for comparison purposes.

Five things to look for when checking the competition:

1. Are they totally honest in their promotions? Do they provide what they say they will?

2. Are they friendly and do they show an interest in you, the customer?

3. Is the product well made or is the service performed satisfactorily?

4. Is the price in line with the worth of the product or service?

5. What is their reputation in the commercial and the residential community?

You are always one step ahead if you know what you are up against. Evaluating your competition makes good sense. To ignore it and just assume that your product or service will be better is business suicide.

Be Open to Change

How disappointing to have this wonderful idea, then after doing all the research you find that the field is too crowded; that there are other products or services too similar to yours for you to be successful. Should you just throw in the towel and give up? Or possibly you should try it anyway and hope for some good fortune?

The correct answer is "none of the above". What you need to do in this situation is to re-think, re-design and re-plan. Take your original idea and work with it, shape it into a new project that will probably be even better than the first one.

Remember Patty Kreamer that I mentioned in chapter one? She didn't start out to be an organizer, but circumstances led her to develop that phase of her business and this has enhanced what she has to offer and was a huge asset in her success.

What can you do, or add, or change, that will make you stand out among contemporaries? Lynn R. Emerson, Esq. of BusinessLegal is an attorney who specializes in working with all aspects of the legalities of business. Lynn said, "I began my own practice because I was frustrated with the "traditional" structure and function of most law firms. Additionally, I was a business person for many years prior to attending law school, and I wanted to utilize my experience."

Frustration and recognition of an unfilled need, plus the added bonus of experience in business was the incentive for a practice of her own where she has seen her efforts pay off in success.

You can do the same. Frustration is often the motivating factor in going into business for yourself. A good example of this is Pat Kaley, owner of Patricia A. Kaley, Secretarial & Word Processing Service. Pat says, "I was fired from a position and knew of a woman who was always trying to sell her secretarial service business. I made arrangements to buy the business, but she backed out just before the closing – so I started my own service."

Pat saw her setbacks as opportunities and thanks the two people she considers to have been most helpful to her. She says they are, "The person who fired me – he had no business integrity and I've made that an integral part of my own business, and the person who decided not to sell to me. I acquired her clients anyway."

So by looking at frustration and disappointment as possible opportunities for improvement you can be motivated to change your focus and reach even greater heights of success than you otherwise would have.

Determination

The success of your business relies on many factors, not the least of which is determination. You *must* believe in yourself and in your product or service enough to keep you from becoming discouraged at pitfalls and unexpected setbacks.

It's so easy to say, "I tried, but it just isn't working, so I quit." It is the determined person who will say, "well, that didn't work too well so I'll try something a little different."

If you have a deep and burning desire for a particular interest, you may try different occupations that will pay more or provide less stress, but at some point that burning desire will burst into flame and you will have to follow your passion. Once that happens, it will take a lot of determination on your part to stick to the project and not take the easier way of working for someone else.

Test the Waters

Just because you are convinced of a great need for your product or service doesn't make it so. Take the time to find out and avoid later disappointment.

The first thing to ascertain is, is there a real need. Ask people whose opinions you trust, to give you honest feedback. Do not rely on family or friends. They will tell you what they think you want to hear because they don't want to hurt your feelings. That will be of no help to you whatsoever. You need *honest* opinions, even if they aren't what you hoped to hear. If you do hear negative comments, don't ignore them, but investigate the reasons for the comments and use that information to change or modify your plans. If all the feedback is positive, be suspicious, nothing is perfect!

After investigating the market, evaluating the competition, and determining that there is a need for your product or service, the next most important question is, will the consumer be willing to pay for what you have to offer.

It's one thing for people to say that you have a great idea and the need is there for it. But when you ask them to pay they might be a little more hesitant. Watch your pricing. Carefully factor in all your costs no matter how minor, then add a small percentage for profit. If this makes the price too high, go back to the drawing board and see what you can eliminate and still provide quality. Try to make the price to the customer as appealing as possible and still make money for yourself. After all, no matter how much you enjoy what you're doing, you are still in business to make money.

I'm sure you have heard the saying that location is everything. This may be just what you need to look at when deciding if you should pursue your dreams in a field where there are already several others who offer the same thing. There may be three pizza shops in as many blocks, but how about five or ten miles away? Or, there may be several established beauticians in town, but what about out of town, or in a mall area? A sandwich shop next to a well-known restaurant may be hard pressed to make a go of it. But what if that sandwich shop was located near a high school? Of course, if you have a home based business there won't be much choice as far as location, however, you can solicit your clients from other areas and possibly offer an incentive for trying your product or service.

To be aware of your competition and of every facet of the business you have decided to pursue is the best preparation you can have for success.

Summary

Careful preparation is the key to a successful business. There are several areas that you need to concentrate on before taking the plunge.

Of course a major concern will be your competition. You need to discover first of all just how much competition you actually have. Listed below are a few places to look for this information.

- The Internet

- Telephone book

- Newspaper advertisements

- Trade magazines

- Trade organizations

- Craft shows and shops

- Word of mouth

Finding a niche market can be a way to increase your customer base. Think of people who you feel would fall into a particular category and focus your marketing on them. The results will speak for themselves.

Discovering who your competition is can be a good start, but then you must evaluate them to see if they will be enough of a threat to you to cause you to re-think your plans.

Be prepared to change your plans to suit the circumstances. There are times when the original idea must be discarded or have drastic changes made to it before you can safely go ahead with it.

An entrepreneur must be a determined person who is not discouraged by setbacks, but rather, uses them to spur her on to see her dreams fulfilled.

Before putting a lot of money into your business find out if it will be accepted by the public. Ask for opinions and weigh each one carefully, noting the positive responses and investigating the reasons behind negative responses.

Keep in mind the five important p's to any situation: Proper Preparation Prevents Poor Performance.

Chapter Three

A Look at the Legal Side

When your idea is new and you are excited and anxious to put everything into motion it can be very difficult to settle down and go through the mundane aspects of what needs to be done on a legal basis. But, it is taking the time now, before you get in too deep, that could save you money and much anxiety in the future.

According to the Western Pennsylvania Small Business Resource Guide, the first thing you have to consider is what the structure of your business will be. You have several choices. Most home based and small businesses use a **sole proprietor** structure. This type of business consists of one person operating a business as an individual. A sole proprietorship is simple to set up and to maintain, however, there are few tax benefits and the owner is personally responsible for all business debts. A business permit is applied for from the county/city clerk in which the business is located.

The next style is a **general partnership**. A partnership exists when two or more people join together in a business venture. This is similar to a sole proprietorship in that it is fairly easy to establish and is subject to little regulation. It is recommended that a formal partnership agreement be drawn up stating the duties and liabilities of each of the partners. By so doing potential problems can be averted before they arise. In a general partnership all profits are taxed as income to the partners based on their percentage of ownership. A general partnership needs to be registered in the same manner as a sole proprietorship.

In addition to a general partnership there is an entity known as a **limited partnership.** In this type of arrangement, a general partner has the freedom to make certain basic decisions, she has unlimited profit potential and so, also, unlimited liability. The limited partner has little or no voice in the running of the business, receives limited profits, and incurs a limited amount of liability in proportion to the amount of their investment. A limited partnership should also be established through a formal agreement that spells out the duties and limits of each partner.

Since most of you reading this book will be a sole proprietor, or become involved in a partnership, I will not go into detail in the more complicated forms of business. But I will let you know what they are and what their benefits and drawbacks consist of.

If you form a **"C" Corporation** your personal assets are shielded from business debts and liabilities. Also benefits are offered to the members. This type of business can be complicated and expensive to establish and to maintain.

A **Subchapter "S" Corporation** takes advantage of a special section of the Internal Revenue Code which permits a corporation to be taxed as a partnership or sole proprietorship and the profits are taxed at the individual rather than the corporate rate. There are restrictions to this form of set up. An explanation can be found in the IRS publication 589.

A **Limited Liability Company (LLC),** or **Limited Liability Partnership (LLP)** are two business forms gaining in popularity. These provide the benefits of corporation, but are less complicated to set up and to maintain.

It would be a wise move at this point to utilize the services of an attorney, particularly one who is familiar with business law.

Lynn R. Emerson is an attorney who has a practice in Pennsylvania and specializes in business law. She has been the source of much of the legal information in this chapter. She does *caution* everyone that, although the laws are similar throughout the country, the advice and information she has provided is based on Pennsylvania law, so each person will have to consult her own state for laws that are applicable to her.

By engaging the services of an attorney at the beginning of your venture she can perform the following for you:

- Make sure you have the right entity for your circumstances.

- Assure compliance with statutes pertaining to each form.

- Draft appropriate shareholder, operating, or partnership agreements to protect each person's interests.

- Draft incorporation documents to assure maximum liability protection for officers and directors.

- Assure compliance with local zoning requirements (especially home-based businesses).

- Counsel sole proprietors on how to title property and the use of insurance to maximize liability protection.

- Draft working agreements with vendors, customers, employees, landlords, lenders, etc, to avoid liability and protect the person's interests and rights.

Basically, a business attorney can get the business started on the right foot.

Other Professionals that are Important to a Start-up

In addition to an attorney, there are several others who are vital to a new, or established business owner.

<u>Accountant:</u> Having an accountant you can trust to handle your business is a basic necessity. Not only can she advise you on tax laws that pertain to your situation, but she can also help you keep accurate records and let you know what is, or is not, deductible as a business expense. Your accountant must be a person with a business sense that meshes with your own. When you find her, take the advice she gives you and your business will be off to a good start.

<u>Commercial Insurance Agent:</u> If you are doing business out of your home you may think that your homeowners insurance will cover any eventuality. That is not so. One example is that if you have a client come to your office and when he is leaving he trips and injures himself, your homeowners insurance is not liable for

the expenses. It is to your advantage to consult with a commercial agent who can make you aware of the special needs of a business owner. This relationship could save you a good bit of money if an insurance related situation occurs. Some possible coverage to consider would be: liability, property, business interruption, "keyman", automobile, officer and director, and home office.

Banker: A good working relationship with a banker who knows you and is knowledgeable about your business can help to pave the way for advice on the best type of loan for you as well as other money questions that are bound to arise as your business grows. (More about money in a later chapter.)

What's in a Name

What's in a name? Plenty if it's the name of your business. What you choose to call your business should reflect the type of business it is. *The Jane Jones Company* tells me nothing about the business Jane Jones is conducting. *Jane Jones Temporary Employment* tells me that if I'm looking for temporary help, Jane Jones is the person I would want to call. *Dipsy Doodle* is cute and catchy, but what is it? Dipsy *Doodle Ice Cream* gives me a better picture of what is being sold. Be very careful and don't be hasty in choosing a name for your company. It could be critical to your success.

After you have decided on the perfect name, do a search to verify that it isn't also the perfect name for someone else's business. Make a call to your state offices, or check the website for your state where you can obtain this information. Once you know that your name will be unique you should protect yourself by registering the name. Again, your state offices will be able to give you the directions on how to do this simple process.

Organizing Your Business Plan

Although it is not a legal necessity to have a business plan, I'm including it here because it is such an important aspect of starting a business.

A business plan makes it necessary for you to think through and examine every detail of your business. You are forced to outline each aspect of starting and operating a financially profitable business.

If you need to seek a loan to get your venture off the ground the lending institution will pay very close attention to your business plan. The plan will also serve as a guideline in future years since you can refer to it to make sure the business is progressing in the way that you intended.

Listed below is a brief outline of how a business plan should be developed. It will be helpful for you to use this as a guide when preparing your own plan.

- **Introduction:** In the beginning of your plan you should provide a detailed description of your business and the goals you hope to achieve. Tell about the type of structure (sole proprietorship, etc.) Anyone reading this plan needs to understand why you feel that you have the expertise to be a successful entrepreneur, so include all the skills and experience you are bringing into the business. The final part of the introduction should discuss the advantages that you and your business have over your competition.

- **Marketing:** The marketing section of your business plan should include such things as a discussion of the products or services you offer and you should also identify the customer demand for your product or service. Write a description of your primary market including the size and location. Give explanations of your pricing strategy and of where and how you will advertise your product or service.

- **Financial Management:** You need to be particularly careful here. If you need to apply for a loan this will be of major interest to the lender. No one will lend you money if you aren't putting in some money of your own up front. So you need to explain how much you have to invest and where it is coming from. To keep expenses in line a monthly budget should be developed for the first year, then updated annually. How much of a return do you think the initial investment will show for the first year? Expand this and provide a projected income statement and balance sheets for a two-year period. What do you think your break-even point will be? Talk about it. Explain how you intend to be personally compensated. What type of accounting system will you use? Will you keep the records of accounts or will someone else have that responsibility? If not you, then who? Consider what financial problems may come up. How would you handle them? Explain as accurately as possible.

- **Operations:** The nitty-gritty day to day running of a business is the factor that can make or break it. Discuss in your plan how this will be accomplished, what will your hiring and personnel procedures include? Have you decided on such matters as insurance, rent agreement (if applicable)? Explain what equipment is necessary and show how you will produce and deliver your services.

Concluding Statement: This is the area where you should summarize the goals and objectives of your business. Remember that your business plan should be examined on a regular basis and should be flexible enough to change as your business grows.

A good business plan is the cornerstone of a successful venture.

Summary

To get started legally on the right foot you must become familiar with the different types of ownership and determine which is best for you.

You should secure the services of an attorney, accountant, insurance agent and banker to be certain of professional help in areas that could become complicated and cause you needless anxiety and worry.

When choosing a name for your business it is essential that you carefully consider how the name will impact your prospective clients. Is it descriptive enough? Will you be happy with it in the future? Try different ideas before making a final decision.

Although not a legal issue, developing a business plan is so important that it has been included in this chapter. A business plan should cover all eventualities and be sound enough to convince a lender that you and your company are a worthy risk. By following the formula outlined, you can form a plan that is workable and that will continue to service as a guideline for future years.

Chapter Four

Money Matters

How much money do you need to start your business? Naturally, there is no one answer that will apply to everyone. Each business has different needs, but there are some expenses that are common to all. Before approaching a lender know exactly how much money you will need to successfully operate your business. Prepare a budget and include every detail, no matter how minor it seems to be at the moment. Those small costs have a way of adding up over a year to an amazing total.

The owner of a limousine service commented on some of the problems she faced when starting her business. She said, "Financing, high maintenance costs and high insurance rates were major issues and continue to be some of my biggest concerns."

To help you to plan for expenses I am listing some of the areas where you may need to factor in your costs for an accurate budget. Not all items will apply to everyone, and you may have some that are specific to your business that are not on the list. But, this guideline should help you to focus your thinking on what your expenses are likely to be.

- **Business licenses and fees.** This will vary with each individual depending on the area in which you will do business.

- **Rent.** If you need to rent a place from which to conduct your business remember that this is a monthly fee, so in preparing a budget for a year the amount must be multiplied by twelve.

- **Utilities.** Will you be responsible for the payment of gas, electric, and water? If so, then these must be included. If you don't know what they will be, estimate on the high side.

- **Supplies.** If you are involved in the manufacture of a product take into consideration all supplies necessary to produce the item. If this is a product you have produced on a small scale keep in mind that you need to increase the amount of supplies used by a considerable amount and this includes any inventory you need to have on hand.

- **Equipment.** Do you need special equipment to produce your product? If you already have some equipment will you need to purchase more in order to meet customer demand?

- **Dues.** It is important to keep abreast of what is happening with others in the same field. To do this it may be necessary to join organizations focused on your specialty, or to subscribe to magazines on the subject. Make a list of what groups you need to join and which publications you need to subscribe to and include the dues or cost of the subscriptions in your expense review.

- **Schooling.** Do you need to take special courses to increase your expertise in your product or service? Find the cost of schooling and include it.

- **Insurance, attorney and accountant.** These three professionals are necessary for your success. The fees for their services are part of your operating expenses and must be part of your list.

- **Advertising.** If you're going to be successful you need to let people know you're there. You can do this through careful use of your advertising dollars. Decide on an advertising budget and enter this amount into your expenses.

- **Clothing.** Will you need special clothing for your business? Do you have the appropriate apparel to meet with clients and with peers? As we will see in a later chapter, a professional image consists of many facets and clothing is one. It need not be expensive, but it does need to be professional.

- **Office equipment and supplies.** Whether your business is home based or run out of a separate office, you need to have equipment and supplies. Make a list along with the approximate cost of each item. Do you need a computer, fax, file cabinets, typewriter, paper, paper clips, file folders, and mailing supplies such as stationery, envelopes and stamps? When starting out ignore the special office items that you would *like* to have and concentrate on those that you *need* to have. The others will come later when you can afford them. Don't forget to include the cost of a telephone and the monthly bills that come with it. It would be impossible to conduct business without a telephone so a telephone free from family use is vital.

- **Transportation.** Do you have reliable transportation or will you need to purchase a vehicle for business use? If you do need to purchase one, this would be a big item to consider.

- **Taxes.** You must have some sort of plan in place to prepare for payment of taxes. You can set something up through your accountant or create a special bank account where you deposit a percentage of your earnings monthly to be used only for taxes when due.

- **Personal money.** It may be months, or even a few years, until your business is making enough for you to take a salary. Do you have enough put aside to live on during that time? It would be a wise move to factor living expenses into your expense list.

- **Additional expenses.** Add on any expenses that are not already on the list and would be unique to your situation.

Does your index sound overwhelming? Don't be intimidated by the total. It is much better to be prepared than to underestimate and find that you can't afford to run your business due to lack of funds.

Now that you know how much money you need you must explore your options to finds the best possible source to help you. Your decision may be influenced by the amount of money you need.

The first place to look for the money you need is through your personal finances, either through savings or other sources such as stocks. Some individuals use a credit card to finance their start-up but considering the interest charged by credit card companies other options may be more desirable even if the amount is not excessively large.

If your personal finances don't meet your needs, try friends and family. They are usually agreeable to help you get the start you need and often do so at little or no interest. If you do get money from friends or family be sure to put in writing how much will be paid back, when the payments will be due, and at what rate of interest, if any. This gives the lender peace of mind and it also makes it binding on you. You won't be so quick to say something like, "I'm a little short this month. I'll skip this month, they won't care." If you agree to certain terms, stick to them. Your reputation is at stake and also you never know when you may want to expand and need their help once more.

Banks and credit unions are the most common sources for loans. When approaching either institution for money you will be far more successful if you can produce a sound business plan for their examination.

There are firms that will help expanding companies to grow. These are called venture capital firms and in exchange for their help they demand equity or partial ownership in the business.

What is the best avenue for you to follow when it comes to finding the money you need? Only you will know for sure. Considering your options carefully will assist you in making the right decision.

It has been said that lending institutions don't like to lend money to small businesses. This isn't true at all. Banks make their money by lending money, but they have to know that the money will be repaid. What causes most small business owners to be denied a loan is not the fact that they are small, but instead it is because they are unprepared when they request the loan. Your request will be denied if the lender considers you to be a high risk. You must convince the lender that you are a good credit risk. The way to do this is through a written loan proposal.

There are basically two types of loans: short-term and long-term. A short-term loan will mature in one year and is used for such things as working capital loans, accounts receivable loans and lines of credit. Maturity dates of long-term loans will be greater than one year, but less than seven years. This type of loan is used for major business expenses. Loans for purchase of real estate and equipment can have a maturity life of up to 25 years.

According to the Western Pennsylvania District Small Business Resource Guide a good loan proposal will contain the following key elements:

General Information

- Business name, names of principals, Social Security number for each principal, and the business address.

- Purpose of the loan – exactly what the loan will be used for and why it is needed.

- Amount required – the exact amount you need to achieve your purpose.

Business Description

- History and nature of the business – details of what kind of business it is, its age, number of employees and current business assets.

- Ownership structure – details on your company's legal structure.

Management Profile

- Develop a short statement on each principal in your business, provide background, education, experiences, skills and accomplishments.

Market Information

- Clearly define your company's products as well as your markets.

- Identify your competition and explain how your business competes in the marketplace.

- Profile your customers and explain how your business can satisfy their needs.

Financial Information

- Financial statements – balance sheets and income statements for the past three years. If you are starting out, provide a projected balance sheet and income statement for three years.

- Personal financial statements on yourself and other principal owners of the business.

- Collateral you would pledge as security for the loan.

When reviewing your request for a loan the primary interest of the lender is repayment. Very often they will order a copy of your business credit history. It is to your advantage to work with the agencies to help them present an accurate picture of your business.

Using a combination of your credit report and the information provided by you these issues will be examined:

1. How much savings or personal equity have you invested in the business? A bank will not finance 100% of your venture. You are expected to provide 25 to 50%.

2. Your credit rating, work history and letters of recommendation will be looked at closely. This is a very important aspect.

3. The lending officer will ascertain if you have the necessary experience and training to successfully operate the business.

4. Your loan proposal and business plan must give evidence of your understanding and commitment to the success of the business.

5. Will there be enough cash flow to make monthly payments?

You can obtain your credit history by writing to Equifax, P.O. Box 105496, Atlanta GA 30348-5496 or call 800-997-2493.

If there are any discrepancies in your credit report take care of them before applying for your loan. Bring any unusual circumstances to the attention of the lender and be prepared to discuss them

This is a most vital step on your path to entrepreneurship. Take your time and be certain to get all your facts together before approaching a lender. Study your information well and be prepared to answer any questions the lender might have.

If you have followed all the guidelines provided you should have no trouble obtaining the necessary funds for your business.

Summary

Before trying to borrow money to start your business you have to know just how much you will need. A list of all likely expenditures, projected through at least one year will give you a pretty good idea.

Banks and other lending institutions make their money by lending money to you. They are more than willing to accommodate you, however, you must do your part by being prepared.

In addition to a detailed business plan, you must present a well thought out loan proposal, have a good credit rating, and be able to convince the lender of your sincerity, experience, commitment and ability to run a successful business.

By following the guidelines given for a loan proposal you will be able to produce a professional and accurate document to present to the lender.

Chapter Five

Making Wise Decisions

The title of this book tells you that your business is yours and yours alone. This means that all decisions rest on your shoulders and your shoulders only. So it is very important that all decisions are thought out carefully and logically because the results can make or break your business.

Becoming an entrepreneur is not to be taken lightly. It requires careful thought and preparation.

When you are planning to take your idea to the public as a business there are several questions you will need to ask yourself.

Is this something I will enjoy doing for the remainder of my working years?

There is too much time and money invested in a business to treat it as a hobby that you can quit whenever you're tired of it.

Am I willing to work long hours seven days a week to make this a success?

It makes no difference how inspired you idea is if you aren't willing or able to put every ounce of your energy into it.

Do I have, or do I know where to obtain, the finances necessary?

Once you have actually begun your business is not the time to discover that you need more money than you have available. Know beforehand what you will need and where you will get it.

Do I have the education necessary?

This may mean additional formal education, or it may mean prior experience. For example: Do you know what is required to keep the books for your company? It may be to your advantage to take a business course at a local college. Community colleges are great places to get the additional education you need. They offer a variety of courses at reasonable costs. Even if it means you must put off the start of your business for a few months it will be well worth it to feel confident and knowledgeable when you do begin.

Is making a large amount of money quickly my primary goal?

Of course everyone wants to see a large profit from their business, but you must understand that this will not happen immediately. It will take time for you and your product or service to become established. It will be up to you to see that you employ the best marketing strategies for your particular type of business. Organizations are a good way to get the word out about your business. Remember too, that you are the best ambassador for your company, so you need to look, sound, and act professional at all times.

No one knows your business as well as you, so trust your own decisions. This isn't to say that you shouldn't gather as much input as you can get. But, after considering all the information you have received you should go through the process of elimination, discarding the useless and considering the useful. If you have done the proper preparation you will know what the right decision will be. Don't be afraid of it – trust yourself. If you are still unsure go to a professional you have confidence in for advice.

Barbara Killmeyer

Graphic artist Christine Manning found that some of her most difficult decisions involve expenditures for equipment. She said, "I have to decide how much money to invest back into the company for state of the art technology that will meet my need to keep competitive while tracking my own market." Christine said that it is also important to keep educated within your field. What Christine likes best about being a business woman is the feeling of achievement she experiences as her company progresses. She also enjoys the pride that ownership provides. She has these words of advice to new business owners, "Be driven. Be passionate about what you do. Take good care of yourself because you *are* the business.

This is one time when you must research and make the best possible choice even if it causes hurt feelings. Leave your emotions for social occasions and make your decisions in a professional, businesslike manner.

The first decision you will have to make will be whether or not your business idea is a viable one. You will have to evaluate the competition; how much competition will you have and can you offer a better service or product; one that will bring enough customers to you to make a profitable business? Your friends and family will probably tell you that your idea is wonderful and you should go ahead without delay. They love you and certainly mean well, but they are telling you what you want to hear because they want you to feel good. This is nice of them, but it doesn't make good business sense. Be diligent in your research. Scour the Internet, search newspaper ads and investigate the offers of your competitors. Only after considering every possibility, and deciding for yourself that this will be a good, profitable business, should you go ahead with it.

Once you have made the evaluation and you have chosen to take the plunge into business you will likely be bombarded with names for your enterprise. Keep in mind that the name must reflect the type of business you own and once again, you must be the one to make the choice. By all means listen to the suggestions offered to you. You never know when someone will hit just the right name, but ultimately it's your business and you must be the one to choose the name for it.

Do you plan to have a partner or would you rather function as a sole proprietorship? In another chapter of this book the various types of partnerships are discussed along with the pros and cons of each. If, after reviewing your options, you feel that it would be an advantage to have a partner, then you must consider carefully whom you choose. Your best friend or a favorite family member is not always the optimum choice. Review the information under Partner: Asset or Liability and make your choice by following the guidelines given.

There may come a time when you will need to hire additional help, either part-time or full-time. If this is the case, and your friend tells you that her teen-age daughter would be ideal for the position, plus it would give her the chance to make some extra money. Beware! Think carefully about what you know of this girl. Is she old enough to handle the responsibility of a job, or is she more interested in dancing, parties, and dating? Perhaps it is her mother who would like to see her with a job, and not the daughter. If you know her to be a reliable and responsible person who would welcome the opportunity to work for you, then of course hire her. If not, explain to your friend that you are seeking someone a little older who would be better able to handle the work involved and who would have the time to devote to the job. Don't allow yourself to be influenced by friendship. The best course of action is to keep friendship and business as two separate parts of your life. By doing that you will be able to keep your friendships and make business decisions that will be advantageous for you.

This same type of situation might arise when choosing your attorney or accountant. Friends will suggest their relatives or acquaintances. You must choose someone you will be comfortable with to handle these key positions. You can't just take a friend's word that her recommendation will be the best choice for you. Make a list of several people for each position, then look into their business background and talk to some of their current clients. These will be important people in your business life and you must make the best possible choice for your needs. Cynthia, an attorney, might be the life of the party and fun to be with socially, but will she give you the best legal advice when you need it? Decisions such as these are never easy to make, but you must trust your own judgment. Take your time and don't allow yourself to be rushed. You will make the right choice if you do the proper preparation.

If you need a location other than your home from which to conduct your business think carefully about where this should be. Perhaps there is a facility within a block or two of your home. This would certainly be convenient for you, but maybe there is a place a few miles away located in a shopping mall, or on a busy highway. You may need to give up convenience to get a place that will bring more people to you and where you will be more easily noticed. Instead of jumping at the first place you see, look into several locations and take note of any repairs or improvements for which you will be responsible. Talk to other merchants in the area to discover what they consider to be the advantages or disadvantages of doing business from that location.

Maintain a positive attitude and don't become discouraged if your business doesn't take off as quickly as you thought it would. It may take longer than you expected, but if you've done all your preparation you will see results. There are some businesses where timing is a factor. For instance, if you open an ice cream shop in January don't expect to see actual profits until at least May. There is a positive side: You will have from January until the warmer weather to let people know you are there, and if you can give some free samples they'll know how good your product is and will see that you are busy when ice cream weather arrives. Give careful consideration to the time of year you will launch your venture. It's very tempting to start as soon as possible, but you may save money if you wait until the timing is right for your product or service to be in demand.

Summary

Before starting your business prepare for it by thorough planning and thought. Ask yourself some introspective questions before making your final decisions.

Keep abreast of the newest trends in your field.

If your education regarding business know-how is lacking in any way, either through formal education or experience, take the time to get the knowledge you need.

Don't allow yourself to be influenced by the remarks and suggestions of friends and relatives. Accept all suggestions and carefully consider each one before making your decisions.

Trust your own decision making skills.

Chapter Six

Partner: Asset or Liability

Starting a business on your own can be a frightening experience. You may feel more confident if you have a partner to share problems as well as successes, but before making the decision to include another person in your plans there are several things you must consider.

The first thing to think about when you move from a sole proprietorship to a partnership is who you would want to have as a business partner.

Let's say that you and Betty have been best friends since grade school and have shared many aspects of your lives over the years. You imagine how great it would be to have her as a business partner, but that may not necessarily be the case. This business idea is yours and although she may cheer you on, she may not be enthusiastic enough to want to make it a big part of her life, and that is essential for a business owner. Betty may be loads of fun to be around, but can she settle down enough to be serious about the business? Does she wholeheartedly believe in the product or service as much as you do, or is she just giving you the moral support of a friend? Does she have the time to devote to making the business a success, or is she so involved with other projects that this would not be high on her priority list? If any of the above make you wonder about Betty as a choice then she must be eliminated from your list of possibilities.

In your mental search the name Jill pops up. You've known Jill for several years and have served with her as an officer in various organizations. She is a "take charge" person who has definite ideas about how things should be done, and she is adamant about doing them her way. You've always gotten along with her and so she may be the one you should approach. No, Jill would not be your best choice. Being a "take charge" person is good in many respects, but not in a partnership. A partnership is about sharing and someone with Jill's personality would find it very difficult to discuss and share ideas. With Jill as a partner you may find yourself in a subordinate role in your own business.

How about Aunt Edna? You know she has enough money to invest in the business, you get along with her well enough, and she has a lot of free time that she could devote to making the venture a success. Have you ever heard the saying that you should never sell a car to a relative? The same usually holds true for going into business with a relative. If anything should go wrong, or if one person becomes overly critical of the other and there is a falling out, it would affect the dynamics of the entire family. There are so many families where one member refuses to attend any function that includes another member that she doesn't get along with anymore. That is a real shame and it isn't worth taking the chance that it won't happen with you.

So, does this mean you should give up on the idea of a partnership? No, not at all, it only means that you must be extremely careful to choose the right person for the position. You need to find someone with whom you get along well, who has the time and money to invest in the business and who is as excited about the prospect as you are. She must have a good work ethic and be open to discussion and sharing.

Karyn Ashley Rok, an attorney who has worked extensively with partnership situations says that having a business partner can be a good thing if it is done properly. She advises that a good partnership provides you with backup in the event of scheduling conflicts; it also provides other ideas and insights to help your business succeed. However, she warns, if not done properly it can be emotionally and financially comparable to a very bitter divorce. Karyn says that there are four criteria to use when seeking a business partner.

1. You must respect and trust her.

2. She must be someone with whom you are able to communicate and who will communicate with you.

3. She must be on the same page as you are as to the direction and administration of the business.

4. She must be willing and able to dedicate the time and finances necessary for the business to succeed.

Karyn has this advice for the woman who is considering a partnership as opposed to a sole proprietorship. She states that you should be very particular about choosing the person or persons who will be your partner(s). You must understand that you will be giving up some degree of control and decision making. Some documents are vital such as a partnership agreement that clearly delineates the terms, individual responsibilities, financial arrangements and a termination clause in the event the partnership ends. There should be regular meetings with the partners to review past actions, status and future actions. She recommends seeking the advice of a lawyer when first establishing the partnership to determine the best fit for your needs. For instance, an LLC or corporation may suit your business better than a partnership. She also suggests contact with an accountant to determine the tax consequences of your choice of business enterprise.

Marlene Smith Pendleton of MS Designs, Inc. agrees with Karyn Rok. Marlene says "My husband was my partner in business for many years. It helped me to have him work on the money issues that I didn't have an interest in handling, and allowed me to have more time to be creative." She also agrees that you must choose someone you can completely trust. Her advice is to find someone who enjoys the business as much as you do, and also someone who compliments your abilities.

Mary Ann Paff of Fidelity Bank says that a partner can provide twice the skills, capital, and support, but it should be a formal, legal, arrangement. She acknowledges that a partnership spreads the risk, but it also dilutes the profits. She suggests that you examine your reasons for seeking a partner.

Her advice is this, "Before entering into a partnership consider the following: How much control are you willing to give up, and are you prepared if your business partner has serious issues such as poor credit, divorce, bankruptcy, etc."

Deciding to form a partnership is a big decision requiring a lot of serious thought, but if you choose to go this route your decision making is not finished. Now you must make your mind up as to which type of partnership is the best for you and your situation.

Following are some common types of business partnerships for your consideration.

General Partnership – In a general partnership all partners share equally in rights, responsibilities, and management of the business. Each partner also assumes full personal liability for debts and obligations incurred by the business. In this type of arrangement one partner can enter into a contract on behalf of the partnership which makes the other partner, or partners, legally bound to the terms of the contract. Any profits realized in a general partnership pass through the owners making it taxable to each individual partner. Any losses also go through each member giving them the ability to offset taxable income from other sources.

Limited Partnership – A limited partnership is made up of one or more general partners and any number of limited partners. The general partner, or partners, bears full responsibility for the management of the business. The limited partners have no part in managing the business. The only risk they incur is their monetary investment in the business and share with the general partners only in profits or losses.

Limited Liability Company (LLC) – An LLC provides limited liability protection for its owners, called members, in much the same way that a corporation does for its shareholders without all the formalities and exacting record keeping necessary for corporations. Members of an LLC are usually not responsible for the debts and obligations of the LLC. An LLC is formed by filing Articles of Organization at the state level. Another advantage of an LLC is that it allows for flexibility when allocating ownership interest among the partners. Ownership interest can be divided in any way decided by the partners without regard to the amount of capital invested by each partner.

Summary

When considering a partnership arrangement for your business there are some important decisions to make before taking this step. You must be extremely careful when choosing the person who will be your partner. She must be someone in whom you have absolute trust, who believes in the business as much as you do and who is willing and able to invest the time and money necessary to operate a successful business.

After choosing the right partner you must then decide which type of business partnership would be the best one for you. Some choices are: general partnership, limited partnership, or a limited liability company. An attorney can help you to decide which entity is best and can draw up a partnership agreement as well as any other necessary papers.

Chapter Seven

The Franchise Option

Do you have a burning desire to be in business but are frightened by the thought of all the start-up know-how you will have to acquire? There can be so many questions and doubts, What if I fail? What if I invest my time and money then find out I don't like it? Don't despair! There is another option for you and that option is to purchase a franchise.

What is a franchise?

Here are some terms that will be helpful to you: The person selling the franchise, such as McDonald's, Dunkin Donuts, or Starbucks is referred to as the *franchisor* and the person who is purchasing the franchise is the *franchisee*. This is how it works: The franchisee pays an initial fee plus continuing royalties to the franchisor for the opportunity of using the trademark, receiving the training and ongoing support in addition to using the franchisor's system of doing business and selling its products or services. This can be a huge benefit to you in that you will avoid many mistakes of new business owners since the franchisor has already perfected the operation of the business through the system of trial and error. A good franchisor will do a thorough market research before agreeing to open a new outlet and this should give you greater confidence that the product or service is in demand in the area you are considering. In addition, you will receive an honest appraisal of the competition you will encounter and advice on how you can make your business different from theirs.

This is a real case of strength in numbers. Economically you will save money because you are buying through a company who purchases in bulk so you will be able to purchase such things as equipment, materials, supplies and services such as advertising at a lower cost. This connection to a franchise is also helpful when negotiating for a location or for lease terms. There are certain suppliers who won't deal with new businesses, or they will reject your business because they feel that your account is too small for them to bother with. This will not be the case if you are associated with a franchise.

For the franchisee the risk of failure is greatly reduced because the franchise has already been proven to be successful. By using a trademark that is recognizable to the consumer you save the cost of creating your own logo and the advertising necessary to make it well known to the public. Don't discount the ongoing training and the advice of experts who are available to you for problem solving.

Is franchising for you?

As with anything else, there is a downside to franchising. If you are a highly independent type of person you may not be happy under the strict operational and specifications required in a franchised business.

Starting any new business is exciting and purchasing a franchise is no different. However, you can't allow the excitement to cloud your judgment, causing you to skimp on proper planning. You must realize that, at least initially, you may be cutting your take-home pay in half and you should be prepared for that probability. You will be doing yourself a tremendous favor if you work with a CPA who will help you to prepare a cash-flow projection before you make a commitment. Be aware of how long it will take before you can break even and turn a profit. Know too what the salary will be that you can realistically pay yourself.

When thinking about your capital investment, keep in mind that most companies have varying ranges when it comes to a fee. These ranges can be anywhere from $2,000 to $100,000 plus, depending on the size of the system. This one-time fee allows you to use the business concept, attend the training program and learn the entire business. There is also an ongoing monthly royalty fee ranging from 2 to 10 percent, or an agreed upon monthly fee.

You can expect additional expenses some of which are:

Your facility or location – It is probable that you may have to purchase land or a building, or you may have to rent a building. If you choose to rent, you will incur the added expense of the monthly lease, plus a one-time security deposit, and leasehold improvements. There are some franchisors who might possibly provide you with an allowance for improvements. Most will advise you of their estimated amount for improvements.

Equipment – Depending on the type of business you enter the equipment needed will differ. It is usually not much of a problem to acquire a loan for the purchase of equipment since it serves as collateral.

Signs – Most franchises have a signage package that the franchisee must purchase. This is actually to your advantage since signage can be a very expensive item.

Opening inventory – Your franchise advisor will let you know what your opening inventory should contain. For most, it will be a two week supply. For a business that requires much more of a complicated inventory the amount will reflect that need.

Working capital – In addition to rent you may have to deposit the first and last month's rent plus a security fee. You will also be responsible for deposits to the electric, gas and telephone companies before they will begin service to you. You will need to have money for the cash drawer for making change, money to pay employees, and money for operating expenses until you have a cash flow. If your franchise relies on charge accounts you will need money to carry you until the customers pay their bills and the money is returned to you.

Advertising Fees – Most franchises require the franchisee to pay into a national fund from which national advertisement fees are paid. This is quite an advantage to you since the advertising done by most companies will result in substantial business for you.

Franchise Disclosure Document

On October 21, 1979 the Federal Trade Commission enacted the Franchise Rule that provides important protection for the franchisee. Under this rule the franchisor is required to make a full disclosure of all information needed by a prospective franchisee for her to decide if she should invest in the company. This document consists of three basic sections. The first 23 sections describe various aspects of the franchise program. The second section shows the audited financial statement of the program. The third section contains a copy of every contract or form you will sign if you decide to purchase the franchise. This must be presented to the franchisee at the first person-to-person meeting where the subject of purchasing a franchise is discussed. It must be at least 10 business days before any contract is signed or any money is paid. This is meant to be a cooling off period allowing the franchisee the opportunity to calmly review their decision before making a commitment. The document presented to the prospective franchisee is called the Franchise Disclosure Document, or FDD, and must contain extensive information about the franchise. In addition, the franchisee must receive completed contracts covering all relevant points at least five days prior to the actual execution of the documents. This is considered another cooling off period and an opportunity for your attorney to go over all documents before you actually sign the contracts.

The FDD is a large document containing both useful and not so useful information. It is worth checking for certain essential information. Following is a list of items you should read thoroughly.

Item 2 – Here you will find background information about the business experience of the officers, directors, and managers of the company.

Item 3 – You will find a summary of the litigation background of the franchisor and the principals of the company.

Item 4 – This item lists any bankruptcies in the background of any of the principals.

Items 5 and 6 – These items are important because they summarize your expenditures such as your initial fee and any ongoing royalty fees.

Item 7 – Item 7 gives, in chart form, a typical total investment by the franchisee. This will be vital information when you are preparing your business plan, or seeking financing. This is information that you need to review with your accountant.

Item 8 – The franchisee will discover in this item restrictions placed on the purchase of supplies and inventory. You can also find here information regarding rebates generated by purchases made by the franchisee and the disclosure of what portion of the franchisor's revenue comes from franchisee purchases.

Item 10 – Here financing is discussed. You will discover if the franchisor will provide financing or if he will make special arrangements with banks or other lenders to help you.

Item 11 – This section outlines the franchisor's obligations to the franchisee and describes required computer equipment purchases and the initial training program.

Item 12 – Item 12 details your territorial rights as franchisee, both inside and outside a designated territory.

Item 13 – The details of the trademark licensed to franchisees are discussed in this section. It is important for you to know if it is federally registered or if the status is registration pending.

Item 19 – This section reveals the sales or profits made by other franchisees. If this section is not completed ask why.

Item 20 – This is a statistical breakdown of the company for the past three years. Listed are the number of new businesses opened during this time, and also how many franchisees have left the company over the same period of time. This item also contains the names, addresses and telephone numbers of current franchisees and of those who have left the company in the past year. Call them. They can give you vital insight into the system.

Do Your Research

To begin your search for the perfect franchise for you it is important to discover some personal things about yourself. You must discover who you are and in what circumstances you are happiest. This will lead you in the right direction when you begin to explore franchises that appeal to you. Here are some possible questions you may want to ask yourself:

1) As a consumer, what business excites you? Do you imagine yourself behind a counter scooping ice cream for happy customers on a hot, summer day, serving hot coffee to warm people up on a chilly, blustery day, or seeing the smiles on the faces of children as they munch on their hamburger and fries?

2) What is your fantasy as a businesswoman? Do you see yourself in person-to-person daily contact with your clients, or would you prefer to be behind the scenes and let employees represent the company?

3) Do you picture yourself in a retail setting taking care of long lines of customers all waiting anxiously to spend their money on your product?

4) Is an office setting your idea of perfect working conditions, or would you prefer to be outside enjoying nature and the fresh air?

5) Would you be more comfortable working from your home so you can be close to your family, or would going to a separate facility give you more satisfaction?

6) Is this a business you want to engage in on a part-time basis, or do you see yourself making this a full-time priority?

Your answers to these questions should give you some insight into the type of franchise on which you should concentrate your search.

Count Your Resources

You can't know where to invest your money until you know how much money you have to invest. The best way to do this is to list, on a piece of paper, all of your investment resources. Make a note of your liquid resources, your cash on hand, any savings you may have including that jar where you've been squirreling away loose change and occasional dollar bills for a rainy day. If you have a relative who has offered in the past to finance your entry into business, now is the time to take her up on her offer. If you know of someone who has come into a large amount of money, don't be shy in talking to them about a business loan. Do you have equity in your house or any other assets that can be used to secure a loan? Write everything down so when the time comes you will have a realistic idea of exactly what assets you have. This will save you much time when it comes to narrowing down your choices for a franchise investment.

The Search is On!

All of the previous information will help you to decide if a franchise is really for you, and if so, which type of franchise you want to explore further. Now is the time to investigate companies in your area of interest to discover which have the most growth potential. Once you have determined the type of company, and the growth potential of that company, check your geographical area to ascertain whether or not a market for that type of franchise exists. This should bring your interest down to just a few choices. Contact the franchises you are interested in and request information regarding the franchise and the purchase requirements. Remember though, that this information is coming from the company so you will need to do some investigating on your own to find out all you need to know.

You can begin your investigation by going online to find any magazine or newspaper articles that mention the company. Read them carefully. Are the articles favorable and is the company depicted as having good management and growth potential?

Another place to explore is the consumer or franchise regulators in your state. Here you can see if there are any serious problems with the company, or if the company or principals have been involved in any lawsuits or bankruptcies. This is important information to have when considering a company in which to invest.

Consult Dun & Bradstreet. If the company in question is a member you may request a D&B report giving you details on the financial standing of the company, payment promptness and other valuable information.

A check with your local office of the Better Business Bureau will let you know of any complaints that may have been filed against the company.

Attend a Franchise Trade Show

By now you should have your search narrowed down to your area of interest and to the investment you are able to make to purchase a franchise, but your investigative work is still not finished. One way to gather a lot of information in a short period of time is to attend a franchise trade show. This is also a good place to compare companies that fall into your range of choices.

Remember that this is just a small sampling of available franchises. Don't waste your time on the companies that are of no interest to you, instead, visit the booths of all that you might be considering. Dress conservatively and ask questions. If necessary, take notes on the answers you receive. Take all handouts offered. Before leaving the booth, give your name and telephone number, or if you have them, leave a business card. Let the operators of the booth know that you are a serious prospect for a franchise purchase and would welcome a follow up phone call. Collect business cards from those who interest you.

After the show put all the handouts you collected into separate folders and read them thoroughly. If there is a company that definitely sparked your interest, don't wait for them to call you, instead give them a call and arrange a meeting with a representative. At that meeting you can ask questions of more depth and also request of copy of their FDD.

Conduct a Thorough Analysis

You have performed all of the above research and decided on a company that seems to be just right for you. Now you must take all the information you have gathered and analyze it in order to discover the following;

1. What is the profitability of the franchisor and of the current franchisees?

2. Is this a growing company that you can rely on to be there for you when you need them?

3. Is the franchise well-organized or are things done in a haphazard manner leaving the opening for errors and failure?

4. Can the company be accepted nationally or is the appeal relegated to one particular section of the country?

5. Is it a well known and accepted company whose name has instant recognition and customer appeal?

6. What is the special difference between this company and its competitors? Why do customers prefer to patronize this particular company and not a similar company?

7. Is the capital investment you are expected to provide reasonable, or does it seem to be out of line with other like franchises?

8. In your investigation into the background of the franchisor did you find his character to be one of integrity and his commitment to be solid?

9. Does the company have a monitoring system to assure the honesty and quality of the franchisees?

10. What purchases are you obligated to make from the franchisor?

11. Does the company have a high success ratio?

Never be hesitant about asking questions or requesting material from the franchisor. Keep in mind that as you are checking them out, they are doing the same to you.

The Franchise Agreement

The franchise agreement is an important document that outlines the obligations of both the franchisor and the franchisee. Uniformity should be ensured for the protection of both parties. The agreement lists what the company expects of you regarding standards of operation, what quality products you will use and the quality services you will provide. The company is expected to provide you with the training, help and goods promised to you as a franchisee. It provides for remedies in the event of defaults and the steps that will be taken by the company if you violate any of the agreed to rules.

Some other information in the franchise agreement includes:

Your use of trademark signage: what you may or may not do with it.

Company provided training, advisory service, and promotional materials

Company approval of any advertising

Your adherence to the operating manual provided by the company and also you are to keep the contents of the manual confidential.

You must maintain the location of your business and keep it in good repair according to company standards.

You must keep accurate records which include weekly sales reports, semimonthly sales reports and monthly profit and loss sales reports. These records must be available for inspection by company representatives.

These sections provide for uniformity including purchases which conform to the specifications of the company.

Quality control of labor intensive products made on the premises which can be food or manufactured items is addressed in the agreement.

You may not change anything without the approval of the franchisor, however, if the franchisor decides on changes he can force you to implement them.

The franchisor will establish the amount and type of insurance you must carry including workman's compensation, general liability, product liability, bodily injury and property damage.

The agreement will also state how long your agreement will be in effect and what options will be available when that time is up.

Time for Visits

Before you sign anything you need to spend some time visiting and asking questions. Your first visit should be to the franchisor or his representative. Be prepared to answer some questions because the franchisor will want to know more about your financial status, your background, and your experience. He must feel comfortable about your representation of his company.

Prepare some questions to ask about the company. It would be a good idea if you would have your attorney check your list to see if anything else needs to be included. Your position at this point will be to determine the strength of the franchise. Here are some questions to help you with the interview.

By this time you will have received an earnings statement regarding the existing franchised companies. Ask for the pretax net profits of these same operations and compare the two.

Get definite answers about what is included in the training program, what field assistance you can expect and what the company's role will be in store design, facility construction, site selection, and feasibility studies.

Ask if any additional working capital will be required after the initial fee investment. If so, find out how much this will amount to.

Request a current price list for supplies to the business.

Find out if there are any plans for company expansion and how any disputes between franchisor and franchisee are settled.

After you have visited the franchisor, or his representative, and had these and any other questions you may have had answered, it is time to see some franchisees to get their opinions and answers to more questions. Once again you should have a list of questions with you when you go. Some things you will want to ask about are:

How good was the training in helping you to get started?

When you have a problem is the franchisor readily available to you for help?

Describe for me a typical day.

Did you encounter any problems that surprised you?

Were there any expenses incurred that you didn't anticipate?

Are your sales consistent or seasonal?

Has this been a positive experience for you and, if you had the chance, would you do it again?

Have any conflicts arisen with the franchisor, and if so, how were they resolved?

Experience Reality

No one can really know what a company is like unless they put in some time and experience the day-to-day hands-on work involved. No amount of research can prepare you for the actual work of owning a business. Ask a current owner if you may work in his business for at least one week at no cost to him. This will give you a true picture of what your days will be like if you go ahead and purchase the franchise.

Summary

This chapter has focused on purchasing a franchise as an alternative to starting a new business from scratch.

Purchasing a franchise can help you to avoid many mistakes made by new entrepreneurs since most of the groundwork has been thoroughly researched by the franchisor. The trademark and much of the advertising has been done eliminating these costly items from your budget. A training program and ongoing advice is available to you to assist you in your start-up and to help you with any problems you may encounter after opening.

However, franchising is not without its drawbacks. It is tightly regulated and has strict specifications so you give up a good bit of control over your own business venture.

In addition, you must thoroughly investigate the franchisor to determine if the company is solid and if the principals are of good integrity and thoroughly committed to the operation.

You will be expected to pay an initial investment fee and continue to pay monthly royalties for as long as you own the business.

You must develop a good business plan and be prepared for any unexpected expenses that might arise. If you need help with a business plan it is wise to consult a professional who will show you how to have a plan to cover all contingencies. A good business plan will make it easier to receive a business loan if that is what you need to do, but it will also help you to stay within your budget and to know your strengths and weaknesses.

If, after careful consideration, you feel that purchasing a franchise is the best option for you, follow each of the steps outlined in this chapter to assure safety and satisfaction in your business venture.

Chapter Eight

Smart Marketing

Marketing wisely can bring you much business. But, marketing can be expensive if you don't make every marketing dollar count. Follow the rules below and you will get the most exposure for your money.

Rule #1 **Seek to be different:** Study your competition and compare it to your own service. Think about what customers would like to have that no one is currently offering, then offer it. Perhaps you sell jewelry, you might offer a free appraisal of any other jewelry owned by the customer, or a free cleaning each year for the first three years. If none of your competitors is offering these incentives you will be ahead of them.

Rule #2 **Make use of satisfied customers:** A testimonial will go a long way in influencing a customer to use your product or service. When you receive a compliment, ask if that person will put their comments on paper. Don't hesitate to ask for this and don't hesitate to use it to your advantage.

Rule #3 **Increase your offer:** Studies have shown that by making your customer an attractive offer at the point of sale you can possibly increase your average sale by as much as 30%. You can suggest an upgrade to a better model, add-on's to the product purchased, or a more detailed service. It is when the customer is giving you money that he is most vulnerable to increasing the sale.

Rule #4 **Show the economy of your price:** Break your cost down to the lowest time increment. Rather than quote only a yearly cost that may frighten some people, let them know that it is "only 75 cents a day, or \$5.25 a week, or \$21 a month. This is a figure they can handle and will make them more receptive to the purchase.

Rule #5 **Sell benefits over features:** Separate the benefits of your product or service (what it does) from features (what it is). People are more willing to buy a benefit than a feature. For instance: Suppose you have a service that will care for pets while the owner is away. That is a feature. The owner will have peace of mind knowing their pets are being well taken care of. That is a benefit. Sell the peace of mind and you are more likely to make the sale.

Rule #6 **Use headlines:** Every ad, sales letter, webpage or email signature should contain a headline for your business. Your headline should always include the biggest benefit you offer. Unless the headline grabs their attention potential customers won't continue to read the rest of the copy.

Rule #7 **Make an offer:** Few people can resist responding to a good offer. Never advertise without one/ the better the offer, the more response to your ad. To advertise without including an offer is a mistake that small businesses can't afford to make.

Become the Talk of the Town

Are people talking about you? If it's your business they're discussing think of it as good old fashioned word of mouth advertising, and that can be the best kind to get. What's more, the price is right. Even a negative comment can be used to your advantage. Perhaps someone, out of curiosity, will try your product or service just to see if what they heard is true. Hopefully, they will have a good experience and will spread the good word squelching the negative talk.

It is impossible to please everyone. But, you *can* please most people if you maintain certain standards in your business.

Gain the trust and loyalty of your customers by proving yourself to be trustworthy. You can accomplish this by doing what you promise to do. In this respect, be cautious about what you claim you will do. Only promise what you know you can deliver.

People always prefer to buy from someone they consider to be a friend. Get to know the people who use your product or service and let your relationship with them be warm and friendly. A word of caution: be sincere when you relate to customers. False friendship, or insincerity, will come through and rather than come to you they will turn to your competition.

Customers today have many choices when they are seeking to buy. They are no longer limited to the local area, but with the aid of the Internet they can shop worldwide. Show your customers that you appreciate their patronage through extra attention such as giveaways or special discounts. For example, I occasionally stay at a resort in an area not too far from where I live. I can be there in a few hours and it is a wonderful place to relax. This past spring I received a card offering rooms during their spring, or slow season at less than half the regular price. This offer was extended to return customers only. I appreciated the offer and immediately made a reservation. This is a perfect example of great marketing. They made a good offer and I accepted it.

Even a sincere "thank you" means much to the shopper. See to it that you, and any of your employees, have a positive, upbeat attitude and a genuine smile when speaking to customers. If, all other things being equal, a person has the choice between a place where they are just another sale, and a shop where they feel they are special, guess which one will get their business.

Instead of looking at each customer as a sale, try looking for ways to help him or her. If they ask for information or advice, give it freely. If they don't get the answers from you they'll go elsewhere and take their business with them.

We are all on the buying end at one time or another. Think about the things that annoy you when purchasing an item. What pleases you enough to make you give the sale to a particular person? Keep these thoughts in mind when you are on the selling side and treat your customer with the respect he or she deserves. The size of the sale doesn't matter. The person who spends $5 must be treated the same as one who spends $5,000. That $5 sale might be the one that returns when she has $500 or $5,000 to spend.

If your product or service is inferior it won't take long for the public to know about it. You can boost sales and keep repeating customers by providing the best that you can. Word of mouth works both ways; it can be your best advertising, or it can be your worst advertising. Your customers expect and deserve the best they can find for their money. It is up to you to see that they get it.

The success of your business will hinge on the satisfaction of your customers. It will be well worth the effort to guarantee their satisfaction with your work. Success is built by one customer at a time, but each of these must be a satisfied customer.

Become a Brand Name

What label is on the ketchup that you buy? What type of transparent tape do you usually buy? When purchasing household appliances how do you identify them? They are all identifiable by their brand names. Now, when individuals are interested in your product or service do they refer to it as they would a brand name? Most consumers will buy a name with which they are familiar. For instance, I associate ketchup with the name Heinz so when I shop for groceries I reach for the Heinz ketchup almost automatically. The same is true of canned soups; my mind, eyes and hand travel immediately to the section reserved for Campbells. I grew up with these names so I'm familiar with them and I know that when I purchase these products I will be satisfied.

This should be your goal; to make your business name a household word so that when your product or service is mentioned it will be referred to by your business name. There are several actions you can take to work toward this goal.

No correspondence should be sent from you without your email address and URL (web address). These are extremely busy times and often people will prefer to email rather than call on the telephone. It is a faster, easier way to get information. If your email address and URL are on everything you send out it will be quickly available and encourage requests for information or sales and will be a simple process. A telephone number and a fax number are no longer sufficient on business cards or letterheads. Today it is important to add your email address and URL. Continue to brand your business in every way that you can and at all times.

It has been said that a person must see your name at least nine times before they know it well enough to do business with you, so the more exposure you have the better marketing it is. This is another reason to encourage email exchanges. Each time you correspond by email your signature line should contain your business information. You can encourage this by making an offer of some kind and have those interested email you for more information. Once you get the correspondence going they will be more receptive to giving you their business.

Press Releases Equal Free Publicity

A well written press release can be your lead-in to a large amount of free advertising. Small community newspapers and publications are always on the lookout for news items and since your information is free to them they will jump at the chance to publish it. If your release is interesting enough for further attention they may even interview you for a long article and run it with pictures.

There is a two-fold trick to getting your press release noticed; first, it must be newsworthy and interesting, and second, it must hit your target audience.

If you sell exotic plants and send a press release saying, "We have the best selection of exotic plants in the city", your release will join the other rejects in the wastebasket. But, if you can say, "Our exotic plants will be used exclusively in the Annual City Flower Extravaganza," Then you have a news item. The newspaper or magazine will want to know more, such as, what kinds of plants? Why were yours chosen? What do they cost? How will they be used? They'll probably want a picture of you surrounded by your plants. This is big-time free advertising.

The second criteria is to hit your target audience. Of course your city newspaper would be good, but not surrounding cities; they won't have the interest. Send your press release to gardening magazines, but not to fashion, or handyman magazines. Sending a press release to the wrong place is a waste of your time and theirs.

The press release must be written in a manner that will fit in with the other copy in the publication.

If properly written, one press release can get you coverage all over the country, or the world. A good release can be used over and over again with minor changes to make it fit the location.

Take advantage of every opportunity to send your press release and get it before the public. Remember, the more often your name is seen the more likely a sale will result.

Write an Ad that Sells

Advertising can be an expensive item for your budget. When you place an ad you want to be certain that you will get the best possible coverage for your money. Try one or more of the ideas below when writing your ad and see the positive response you will receive from readers.

1. Your target audience will consist of individuals with varying degrees of knowledge and need. Supply them with different examples that will hit home with each one on the level they will understand. Examples can pinpoint areas in which each potential customer can relate.

2. Prove your expertise by using terms familiar to your field and explaining these terms so that the person reading your ad will be aware that you know what you're talking about and can be relied upon to give good advice and service.

3. Enthusiasm breeds more enthusiasm. You cannot expect others to be excited about your product or service if you aren't. Show through pictures or words how excited you are and what a wonderful opportunity you feel this to be for everyone. Let your own ardor carry over to your readers.

4. Show empathy for your readers. Give them an opportunity to form an association with you by relating to them how you were once in the same position that they are in now. Then explain to them how your product or service pulled you from that position and helped you to reach your present state.

5.   At the end of your ad, backup your claims with a promise of "satisfaction guaranteed or free replacement". The reader will have more incentive to try your product or service if they are assured that you will stand behind your claims.

6.   Everyone would rather be talked "with" than talked "to". Ask questions in your ad. People will automatically answer them mentally and become involved, spurring their interest in your business.

7.   Consumers prefer to do business with people they feel that they know. Introduce yourself in your ad and tell them about you. If they can relate to you they will have more confidence in your business and are more likely to purchase from you.

8.   Begin your ad with a story. People begin to read the story, become caught up in it and forget that they are being sold to.

9.   Don't throw more information at your audience than they can absorb. Five points are the most you should include. Any more than that and the reader will get confused and quit reading the copy.

10. Make reading your ad a positive experience. You can do this through education or even by telling a joke. Whatever avenue you use, make it something they will enjoy and they will look favorably on your business as well.

Practice writing your ad until you have a finished product that pleases you. If you find that you can't do this, then invest in a professional writer to create the ad for you. The money that you spend will be returned many times over by the number of sales generated.

Work That Room

Never leave home without your business cards. Have them with you at all times. You can meet a potential client anywhere and you don't want to miss the opportunity for a sale because you didn't have your cards. The prospect may forget your name and other important information.

Businesses and organizations often host "mixers" where the idea is to meet other business people and possibly make connections that will benefit both parties. If you are shy, introverted, or this is the first time you are attending a function of this type, it can be a terrifying experience. But with proper preparation you will be able to enjoy the event and make valuable business contacts. **Never decline an invitation to a mixer or you will be passing up a priceless chance to put your name into the marketplace.**

Follow these guidelines and the next invitation can provide you with new clients for your business.

Presentation statement – Take the time to prepare a 15 second statement about your business to be used when meeting a new person. For instance, after a firm handshake, you can say something like, "Hello, I'm Cindi Smith, owner of the Tea and Talk Lunchroom. It's good to meet you. What do you do?" This will give the other person an opportunity to introduce herself and her business.

Dress appropriately – Pay attention to the kind of event this will be and dress to fit the occasion. An after work event will require business attire, an evening affair will find people dressed more formally. There are times when the situation is theme related. If the invitation is to a barbeque you would look completely out of place if you arrived wearing clothing that would be more suited to a dinner at the country club. Avoid fad clothing or a garish look. You may want attention, but not that kind. It is better to wear something that is understated and set off with one or two tasteful pieces of jewelry. By dressing in an appropriate manner you will feel confident and self-assured. This confidence will carry you through the entire event. Imagine entering a room full of well-dressed professionals when you are wearing super casual clothing. Your confidence will immediately be eroded and you will be able to accomplish nothing. At the same time, the image that any possible clients will have of you will not be a good one and will not be conducive to selecting you or your business.

Business cards – You should have a supply of business cards with you at all times. Never push your cards on anyone, but rather, discover in your conversation if they have an interest in talking to you further about your product or service. If this is the case, then offer your card and ask for theirs as well. It is good to jot down on their card a short reminder of where you met, the date, and any other information that will jog your memory when you follow up with a telephone call. A useful hint is to wear something with pockets and keep your cards in the right hand pocket and the cards you receive in the left. In this way your cards will be handy and you won't need to be fumbling through your purse to dig one out when you need it. By keeping them in separate pockets you will keep all those you receive together to go over at a later time and they won't get mixed up with yours.

Circulate – Avoid spending most of your time with one person, no matter how interesting they are. You will miss the chance of making many more contacts by staying only with one individual. If they do capture your interest and you would like to get to know them better, suggest getting together at another time for coffee or lunch. You will sometimes find that a guest will stick to you, either because she is interested or because she is shy and feels that she's found a haven. In this case there are two possibilities for you: You can make your getaway by saying, "It was great meeting you. I see someone across the room that I must talk to." Then go to someone across the room and talk to them. Or, you can make your way to someone you know, introduce your new friend to them, and leave them to talk while you continue to circulate.

Leave your friends at the door – If you arrive at the party with a friend or colleague, ***don't stay together!*** Separate and move through the room independently. You will both make more contacts and you will be more approachable alone. Being with a friend can act as a crutch and prevent you from exploring the possibilities by yourself. When you leave you can once again pick up your crutch and discuss the party and the contact each of you have made. But while there – be a loner, it pays.

Alcohol and business are a bad combination – Although alcohol is almost always served at such affairs you need to watch how much you drink very closely. One look at a person who has had too much to drink and any positive thoughts that may have been generated are immediately erased. If you do drink, there are several methods to keep it under control. You can carry the same glass with you the entire time and sip from it very slowly. In this way you can avoid refills, or have just enough missing to fill it with only a small amount. Another method is again to keep your glass and after you have emptied it, quietly refill it with a soft drink and continue to drink soft drinks. Either way will keep you from overindulging and ruining your image.

Follow up – The business cards that you collected at the mixer will do you no good if you don't follow up on them. Within a week of receiving them, choose a day to go over all cards and, after reading the notes you jotted on the reverse of the card to refresh your memory, begin to telephone. Never be pushy, but say something like, "Hi John. This is Mary Fisher. We met last Friday at the networking mixer. I'd like to talk to you further about my service and was hoping I could make an appointment, at your convenience, to meet with you." If the answer is in the negative, be gracious and offer to call at another time.

Attendance at a networking event can be a boon to your business. Take advantage of every opportunity and prepare yourself well so you can make the most of the situation.

Business Exposure Through Organizations

I can't emphasize enough the importance of joining organizations related to your field, and of being an *active* member. I have received more support, learned more about my work, and received more sales, or leads resulting in sales, from members of organizations than from any other source.

You may hear some people say that they joined an organization and then left it because they got nothing out of it. I would be willing to bet that they also put nothing into it.

You can receive something different from each group. One may help you to learn more, another may provide you with leads, and still a third may give you support when your spirits are sagging. Each is important and each is necessary.

Barbara Killmeyer

I first discovered the value of organizations while working in a one-person office. I was secretary to three men and handled all other office duties as well, including a payroll for several hundred people. I worked alone and had no contact with other secretaries. Then I was introduced to PSI (Professional Secretaries International). Joining PSI changed my life. I suddenly had others who did the same work as I did so they understood any problems I had. I made some very good friends, some I still have as friends now, more than 20 years later. By being actively involved in the chapter, I became an officer, then proceeded to the Division level and rose through the offices to become the President of the Pennsylvania Division. All of this served to make me a more confident person, giving me the opportunity to speak before large and small assemblies and develop my leadership skills. It was necessary for me to travel to many of our states and so my horizons were expanded as they never would have been without PSI.

As my career changed I became part of other organizations and each has given me much to be thankful for in different ways.

Don't neglect the opportunities for contacts that can be made through local organizations that are not necessarily connected only with your field of business. Your local Chamber of Commerce, for instance, can provide key business leads.

Summary

Your marketing strategy can actually make or break your business. You want to spend your money wisely and yet you need to get word out about who you are and what you do. By following the seven rules described in this chapter you will be well on your way to smart and effective marketing.

In addition to the seven rules there are several other tactics you can use to increase your prominence in the market place.

If you can become the talk of the town through satisfied customers as well as being known as a friendly, trustworthy person who will do everything they can to please customers, word about you will spread and bring in more business. A word of caution: If you fail to impress people with your friendly, caring manner, or show yourself to be untrustworthy, that will spread too.

Get your business name so well known that when your product or service is mentioned yours will be the one remembered. You must become a brand name and some ways to do that are by making sure your business name is on all correspondence, including your URL, email address, telephone and fax numbers.

Make sure your local newspapers are aware of any changes to your business. You can do this through press releases. If you are expanding, if you are moving to a new location, if you have received an award of any kind, if you plan to speak to any groups, any of these can be reasons to send a press release. There are many more occasions when a press release can be used to get you free publicity. Take advantage of this and you'll see a measurable increase in business.

When you decide to spend money on an ad make it one that will bring the best possible coverage. Keep your target audience in mind and write it like an open letter to them. Show your expertise in the subject as well as your enthusiasm. Your promise of "satisfaction guaranteed" will entice people who are not currently customers to give your business a chance. Keep your copy to five main points; enough to capture their attention but not so many that they will become confused.

Any gathering from your high school reunion to a Chamber of Commerce meeting is an occasion to work the room and make new contacts. Come armed with your business cards, a friendly smile, and a positive attitude. Above all else, circulate! Dress appropriately for the group and have a 15 second statement prepared about you and your business that you can use when meeting other guests. Be conscious of the amount of alcohol you consume. It is never a good idea to mix alcohol and business. You want to make the best impression possible and alcohol will keep you from doing that. Within a week after the event follow up on any business cards you received. Be polite, remind the other person of where and when you met as well as what your business is. Suggest a lunch or meeting at their convenience to discuss possible business.

Join and become active in business and trade organizations. The contacts and experience you receive from these organizations are priceless and should be cultivated.

Chapter Nine

Your Attitude for Success

I'm sure you have heard of the many ways a positive attitude can work for you. This is especially true if you are in business.

If you contact someone to do some work in your home and the person you speak to leaves you with the impression that *he* is doing *you* a favor by agreeing to do the work, is he the type of person you want to deal with? What if you walk into a clothing store and the sales person acts as though you are bothering her, especially if she is on her cell phone and you are interrupting her call? Will you go out of your way to shop there again?

It is always more inviting to be around a pleasant person who has a positive, upbeat attitude than around someone who seems to be unhappy, or grouchy.

How often have you left someone's company and said, "Wow! She sure needs an attitude adjustment!" No one can be happy all the time, but we can control our attitude when we need to do so. There are several methods we can employ to give us the attitude we need to have whether for business or for personal times.

1. Your attitude for the day can be determined before you ever get out of bed in the morning. When you awake you have two choices: You can either say, "Good morning God" or, "Good God, morning!"

2. Start your day with soft, calming music. Leave the television with its loud, blaring commercials and its stream of bad

newscasts off until later when you can handle that. Also, if you use an alarm that wakes you to music, be sure to set it for a station that plays soft music and not one that plays loud Rock or Rap songs. You don't need to be jarred out of your sleep. If this happens you'll be disagreeable for the rest of the day instead of feeling happy and relaxed.

3. Surround yourself with positive, upbeat people who will pass their good feelings on to you. We all know people who can bring us down just by being in their company. Avoid them, even if you are related to them. You don't need to be put into a bad mood.

4. Feel good about yourself. Our brain is constantly giving us feedback about our own thoughts. Most of the time this feedback is negative. If you can change "I'm going to mess this up" to "I'm well prepared and I'm going to do a fantastic job and have a wonderful day" you will have that wonderful day and your confidence in yourself will show through to everyone you meet.

5. Be welcoming. It doesn't matter if you are going to the client's home, or if they are coming to you. Be sincere in your welcome to them. Sincerity cannot be faked. A smile and a cheerful "Hello. How are you today?" if it comes from the heart will go a long way in promoting goodwill.

6. Keep your bad day to yourself. If you spread gloom and doom people will shy away from you, and that is the last thing you want to happen. Instead, if you're having a bad day, and we all have them from time to time, concentrate on any good that has happened, or that you expect to happen, and present that attitude to your customers.

7. Don't be afraid to ask for help. You aren't a superhero so don't try to act like one. Carrying so much on your shoulders can bring anyone down in their mental attitude. If you need help get it as soon as possible. You may need to see someone professionally to help you to cope, you may

need someone to take over for a while to give you a break, or you may have financial problems that are becoming too burdensome. Any of these can affect your attitude turning you into a person who is avoided. If you need help in any area, ask for it. You will be amazed at the number of people willing to give you a hand, and how having such worries taken care of will improve your outlook on life and your attitude toward others.

Your attitude says a lot about you as a person and if you want to succeed as a business person then you need to develop and put forth the best possible attitude. This isn't something you can afford to turn off and on. You never know when or where you will meet a prospective client. After meeting you, do you want them to say, "I think I would enjoy doing business with her" or, "My money is good anywhere, I don't need to spend it on someone with her attitude?

If you are serious about having a successful business, then you need to work on developing a positive attitude that will infect others with your enthusiasm and love of life.

Summary

Attitude is one of the cornerstones of a successful business. An attitude adjustment is something we all need from time to time so work at making yours positive and welcoming.

Do what it takes to start your day on a calm and positive note

Surround yourself with positive people

Learn to feel good about yourself

Be welcoming

Keep your bad day to yourself

Ask for help if you need it

Your attitude is something that is with you 24 hours a day and you never know when you will meet someone who will become a client, so keep your attitude positive and your reputation as a good person to do business with will spread.

Chapter Ten

Put Your Best Foot Forward

Most people believe the saying "What you see is what you get", so it follows that if they see two people; one who portrays a casual, fun type wearing too much make-up and the latest fads and the other looking neat and professional the professional will get the client every time.

Unfortunately, the image you project is not how you see yourself, but how others see you. Your image not only consists of how you look, although that is important, it is also made up of how you speak and how you act. These three components: how you look, speak, and act is what people see and how you will be judged.

How you look: Your overall appearance says so much about you that you should be aware of it at all times. Starting from the inside out, eat properly and exercise regularly to stay healthy and eliminate any signs of illness that can rob your body of a natural glow. An added benefit is that if your skin has a clean, natural beauty you can cut back on the amount of cosmetics that might give it a heavy, theatrical look. Practice good oral hygiene keeping your teeth clean and your breath fresh. You can look your best, but if, when you speak a stale reminder of your last meal fills the air you've already lost that client. When was the last time you had a consultation with a hairdresser to discover the best style for your features? Too many women are told sometime in their twenties that their hair looks great and so they stay with that style for the rest of their lives. Just like clothing, hair styles change, but not everyone can wear the latest. Find a hairdresser whose opinion you trust and follow her advice. After you have a style that suits you, you must keep your hair clean and well groomed. The best cut in the world will look bad if your hair is dull and lank.

Take a good look at your clothes closet. Is all your clothing appropriate only for after hours fun or do you have an adequate number of outfits that are professional and suitable for business? It doesn't matter what your business consists of, no one will take you seriously if you don't look professional. You may feel that you can't afford a professional looking wardrobe, but that is not true at all. If you know what kind of clothing to look for you can find excellent buys at places such as thrift shops, second hand stores, and even estate sales. For just a few dollars spent at places such as these you can put together several smart looking, professional outfits that will carry you through many meetings. Be careful of over accessorizing. A simple skirt, or pair of slacks, paired with a plain blouse and blazer will look great with some tasteful jewelry, such as a plain gold or silver necklace, small tasteful earrings, and a pretty brooch. But, accessorize with large, chunky, pieces that are the latest fad and you will ruin the entire effect. Remember that simple is always better.

How you speak

Have you paid attention lately to the way you speak? Is your language peppered with slang, and even worse, cussing? You don't want your speaking to appear stilted, or snobbish, but if you are careful about your words and grammar you will be perceived as someone who is careful about business also. Some common mistakes that will brand you as a careless person are:
I seen her yesterday,
She don't know the answer,
When is you going to finish that?
He had went to the movies.
Alls you need to do is...
I don't got any of that.
Anyways, this is what I do.
I'll take three of these ones.

Your speech carries over to your telephone persona. When you answer your telephone please speak slowly and clearly. How many times have you called a business office only to hear something like: Good morning, thisisjonesaccountingservice. You aren't even sure you dialed the right number because the name of the company is rattled off so fast. You may answer the telephone many times during the day, and to you, because you know what you are saying, the name sounds perfectly clear. But to the person hearing it for the first time it is a blur and confusing. This can easily be a turnoff for a prospective customer.

How you act

When you enter a room, does everyone know you are there by the boisterous way you made an entrance? Do you make it a point to flirt with anyone of the opposite sex? If alcohol is involved, do you make sure to get as much as you can and end the evening by becoming intoxicated and obnoxious? Do you demand attention by being loud and talking over everyone else? These actions are all sure to produce a negative professional image, not the positive one you are seeking. When you enter a room, smile and greet your host or hostess. Project a positive attitude as you meet and greet the other guests. You want to leave them with the idea that they would like to see you again, and, if they are in the market for your product or service, they want to do business with you.

Summary

Your professional image is important to success and it consists of how you look, speak, and act. Dress as appropriately as possible. Business attire can be purchased reasonably at thrift and secondhand stores. Take care of your health and practice good hygiene. Pay close attention to how you speak and strive to eliminate any slang and cussing from your speech. Practice speaking slowly and clearly using good grammar. Always act in such a way that you will leave a positive impression on others. Be mindful on how loudly you speak, how much alcohol you consume, and what your attitude is with others. By being careful of the above your professional image will be positive and possible clients will look forward to doing business with you.

Chapter Eleven

A Trustworthy Reputation is Beyond Value

Word of mouth can be one of your greatest assets, or it can doom you to failure. Customers who are satisfied and feel that they have been treated fairly will quickly spread the word about your business to family and friends. The same is true of those who feel that they did not get what was promised and deemed you to be untrustworthy. This information too will be passed on to others ruining your reputation and your business. The formula for customer satisfaction is simple: Do what you say you will do.

Here are some examples of good business practices to employ if you provide a service in a clients home:

The number one issue is that of time. If you tell a client that you will be at her home at 9 a.m. be there promptly at 9. If you are unavoidably detained telephone and let her know you will be late and the reason why this is so. To just show up late shows a lack of respect for your customer as well as poor discipline and poor business acumen on your part.

Do your job plus a little more. If you have a house cleaning business do what you have contracted for – then do just a little more. If you are a party planner, plan the best event you can, then throw in something extra, perhaps balloons or a small door prize. If you own a business where your customers purchase items from you, give them a money-back guarantee, then follow it up in a friendly, sincere manner. Be sure what you sell is top quality and your customers are getting their money's worth. These won't cost you a lot of money, but this type of action on your part will go far in gaining you a trustworthy reputation.

Believe wholeheartedly in the merchandise or service that you offer. After all, if you don't think it's the very best how can you expect others to think so.

Be aware at all times of your attitude. Too often when we are shopping we get the impression that the business person feels that he is doing you a favor by providing his service or product. Attitude is all important. No one likes to do business with someone who is grouchy, or in a bad mood. Leave your problems at home and greet your customers with a sincere smile and a friendly welcome. They will enjoy doing business with you and will be likely to tell others what a pleasure it is to buy from you.

If you always do your best for your customer they will come to trust you and will return again and again to give you more business.

Summary

Your reputation as a trustworthy business person is the most valuable asset you have in being successful.

At all times be honest and fair to your customers. Have a positive attitude and greet them in a friendly and sincere manner. Offer only top quality service or products which you yourself believe to be the best.

If your customers know that you will back up any claims with a smile they will let others know about you and your business will swell.

The bottom line is: Do what you say you'll do and do it when you say you will do it.

Chapter Twelve

Advice from Successful People

People who have been successful in business are happy to share what they have learned with those who are just starting on the path to entrepreneurship. Their thoughts about what they learned on the path to good business will help you to avoid some of the same mistakes and give you ideas for new and innovative ways to approach your own journey.

Joy Klohonatz is a direct sales representative for Southern Living at Home, a home party plan division of Southern Living Magazine. She says that she had been a subscriber of the magazine for years and heard they were launching this new division. She said, "Knowing their reputation, I just had to try. I also had just moved to a new area and wanted an opportunity to meet great women." Her greatest help when she started was God and her inner drive. Of course there were problems, and Joy's biggest problem was getting to know the direct sales/party plan industries. She says that what she knows now that she wishes she had known when starting is that it's all a numbers game. The more you talk the more customers, hostesses, and consultants you will be able to serve.

Her advice to women just starting out: "Don't ever hesitate to share. You never know who's life you can change or just make better."

Carole Jo Babish, CLU, CHFC is a registered investment advisor dealing in financial services, insurance, and investments. She has been working in this business for 26 years and said, "I went into this business kicking and screaming. But, I had few other options;

I was divorced, alone, and needed benefits. I had interviewed for other positions and didn't like what was available, nor did I have the money or time to go back to school. So, when this opportunity came my way I, very much afraid of failure, took the chance.

Carole said the men in her office were actually the most help to her. She said, "They wanted me to succeed and mentored me all the way. There were only a handful of women in the field at that time, so no female mentors were available."

Because she did not come from a background of a "natural market" she had to generate all of her business leads. She did this through bulk mail to specified markets such as doctors, lawyers, homeowners, funeral directors, nurses and real estate sales forces. She used telephone solicitations, made 'cold calls' either by phone or in person. Carole did a lot of public speaking to interested groups and joined both social and networking groups. An unexpected problem was that she did not have enough capital to tide her over the days when no commissions came in. She said, "$5,000 more in the bank would have made a difference."

She wishes she had known when just starting that you shouldn't let your fears stop you. Carole said, "If you fall, so what? Just get up each day and "show up". You <u>will</u> succeed.

Her advice to women just starting out: Be confident and let it show. Research – research – research. Ask – ask –ask for help, for knowledge, for favors, discounts, anything you need and everyone you meet. Go to every event you can find. Let people know who you are and what you have to offer. Do what you can for others when you are able.

Elizabeth Babcock, LCSW, LLC is a psychotherapist with a focus on wellness education. She went into business for herself because she said she had concluded that she could no longer be happy working for someone else, and she would have to open her own practice if she was to stay in the profession of her choice.

Her best help was her own careful observation of how a business of this type is run while working for someone else. She noted what advantages and disadvantages there seemed to be for owners of such a business. She also made sure she was well aware of the daily to-do's, irritations, surprises, and challenges of running a business of this type. "Finally," she said, "I did a thorough walk-through at my previous place of employment, making a list of every conceivable item that was necessary to operate the business, from post-it notes to multi-function machines and everything in-between. As a result, I had absolutely no surprises of this nature when I did my shopping and set up my own place." She also had several detailed information interviews with a therapist she knew who has run her own solo practice for some time. She was able to answer every detailed question and make knowledgeable suggestions. Information from her gave Elizabeth a nice head start in getting her practice off to a smooth start.

One of her start-up problems consisted of the many bureaucratic hoops to jump through. Most of these became visible one at a time. She said, "There's no coherent source of information for 'here are all the official organizations you have to register with, comply with, etc,' and yet you, as an owner, are legally responsible for somehow figuring it out and getting it all done. I found that one thing tended to lead to the next, and in the end, nothing major was missed."

She found the scheduling delays and low quality workmanship in the office that was being set up for her to be frustrating, in spite of floor-plan drawings and other planning being done months ahead. For example, a wall was put up in the wrong place and if she hadn't noticed it she would have been stuck with it. She had to be very assertive about everything related to her rental space and specifically ask for what would seem to be obvious things, such as, "Could I have the light switch next to the door instead of five feet away in the middle of a wall?"

Elizabeth wishes she had known how very proactive, assertive, and bull-doggish she would have to be about work done by others that she was paying for. She also wishes she had known how long it would take to get comfortably established as far as local business visibility was concerned. She had planned for two years and it took four. This was difficult for her morale.

Her advice to women just starting out: Research it to death before you start. This will help you to figure out whether you really want to do it at all, and if you do decide to move forward, you'll do so much more effectively and painlessly.

Talk to others who are doing what you want to do. Learn as much as possible about what to expect, good and bad, what works, what doesn't work, and little tips that you could only get from someone who's been there.

Exploit the used office-furniture market. There are huge savings to be had on nice looking furniture if you have the patience to wander through a warehouse that also includes not-so-pretty stuff.

Be very specific and assertive about any space that you rent. Once the workers have left and you've moved in, you will be stuck with it just the way it is for the remainder of your time there. So don't be shy about making them do it right in the beginning.

Communicate with others who rent from your landlord, especially when it comes time to renew your lease. There can be background developments going on that would affect your decision if you knew about them. They may also affect your desire to stay there and also give you bargaining power for your new lease payment.

Be prepared to work harder than you expect, for longer than you'd think. It helps a lot if you've managed to figure out what you love to do, as the passion for the work will propel you through it.

Be assertive and timely about getting payment from clients. The longer the money is outstanding, the lower your chances are of ever seeing it. Be matter of fact about collecting what you are owed, when it is due. They wouldn't ask the grocery store to let them pay later, and they shouldn't expect that of you either.

Network with other people who also serve or have exposure to your target customer population. Develop mutually trusting relationships with them, which will generate referrals.

Get yourself into the news whenever possible, whether it's by writing a letter-to-the-editor on a recent news item of relevance to your business (always identifying your business name, type, and location – the paper will always include this), or getting interviewed by journalists doing a piece for which you have relevant information. This is better than any advertising you can buy. Learn how to write press releases and get contacts from all your local news media for sending them. Do them properly or they won't get looked at, much less printed.

A website is a hugely good thing these days, especially if you set it up in a manner that shows your expertise rather than simply being an on-line ad for your business. I've used mine to showcase my educational articles and workshops, which has given me lots of credibility with site visitors and has resulted in increased business.

Subcontract or hire only people you feel thoroughly good about, in terms of trusting them and liking the quality of their work. The entrepreneurial thing is enough work without having to drag along someone who is not contributing adequately to the forward progress of the effort.

Stay flexible and adaptable, because things will always change, and if you can't change with them, you probably can't succeed.

Karen McCrory is the owner of Estate Transition Services, a business involved in household downsizing of contents due to moving or death in the family.

Karen was laid off from a sales job and she was frustrated with the corporate world, especially their marketing practices. Her parents were elderly and she had to place them in an assisted living facility. This was when she realized the need for downsizing services.

At the time Karen started her business she belonged to a networking organization of women called The Women's Business Network. She said they were very supportive of her and most of her business comes from this organization. Karen said, "In addition, because I have a sales background, I knew how to go out and make sales calls and zero in on my target market. My ability to be a good networker helped me find the expertise I needed when I had questions."

Karen encountered the usual major problems such as needing money to keep the bills paid while she built the business. To address this problem she got a second job on a twilight shift that included benefits. She was able to build her business during the day and work the twilight shift at night.

Her advice for women just starting out: Join a network organization that is supportive. Also, form a group of people with whom you can meet on a regular basis who can offer advice, help you keep your goals, etc. This will be your own personal board of directors.

Anna Marie Petrarca Gire is the owner of Hot Flash Media Inc., a publishing business. She is the owner/publisher of a newspaper, *Women's Independent Press* and also of *The Women's Yellow Pages.* Formerly from Illinois Anna Marie now lives in Pittsburgh, Pennsylvania and she says, "There are no other publications in Pittsburgh that focus exclusively on women's issues in the manner that Women's Independent Press did (and the web site will continue in that fashion), and Women's Yellow Pages does. By providing a uniquely female perspective, our publication is able to transcend age, race, socio-economic background, political affiliation and sexual orientation. The publication was inspired by the lack of serious print media available to women."

Anna Marie conceived the idea for Women's Independent Press (WIP) during a conversation with a friend who was planning to relocate to another city. She considered the difficulty of finding friends or activities in a new place and thought about how convenient it would be to have a printed guide available that listed clubs, resources and activities to help people get acclimated to a new location.

After pondering the idea for about a year she mentioned it to a colleague who embraced the idea enthusiastically. Then they got serious. After several months of planning and endless cups of coffee, what began as a small resource guide blossomed into a 24 page newsmagazine dedicated to women and their vast and varied interests. They named the company Hot Flash Media and the new publication, Women's Independent Press (WIP) was launched in March of 2003 – Women's History Month.

The original idea is now an online newspaper filled with the same high quality of writing and subject material as appeared in the printed version of WIP. In addition, there is a Women's Yellow Pages (WYP) in Pittsburgh that evolved from the original newspaper, which unfortunately had to cease publishing in April of 2005. WYP provides comprehensive information on a variety of subjects, as well as a directory of mostly women owned businesses.

Anna Marie says, "There are a number of women's publications that speak to how to make one's self better on the outside. WIP speaks to who we are on the inside. Women want to read substantive information, to be able to make better decisions about their lives and their community/country. WIP provides that information from a diverse pool of writers, both locally and from around the world."

Of course there were challenges that had to be overcome such as: how to meet deadlines and how to attract advertisers. Anna Marie says that WIP has been, and continues to be a learning experience for her. There are continued financial challenges, always a struggle to come up with enough money to continue with the business, but she says there have been several reinventions of the business which keeps it fresh and visible.

Anna Marie wishes she had learned beforehand more about the publishing business. She also would have looked closer into the financial aspect of the business and she would have made an earnest effort from the beginning to assemble a sales staff.

There were several things that helped her to get started and she is thankful for each of them. A printer in Illinois gave Anna Marie and her business partner a great deal of advice and information on printing, layout, and design. Many writers and editors from around the country gave advice on their experiences with publishing and on where to find writers. She spoke with several women publishers around the country and they gave her advice on different aspects of the business. Many friends gave input in content for the paper and they still give her advice and support for the online version of WIP. She sought advice from the Small Business Administration and in addition, the University of Illinois MBA program took on WIP as a project and provided her with a helpful analysis of WIP in the form of a 500 page document. "But," she says, "the most important help was a passion and excitement for WIP."

Her advice to women just starting out: Starting a business involves more than a great idea, but a great idea is a good place to start. There are many reasons to go into business, including freeing up your creativity, being your own boss, and being able to invest the experience that you have built up over the years into something that is your passion.

After the idea takes root, the next steps are research and planning. It s important to make sure that there is a need for your idea. Some questions to include:

- Do I have competition?

- Is my idea better than my competition? (Of course it is!)

- Who am I trying to reach?

- Do I have the skills for this?

- Who/what are my resources?

- Will this be a for-profit or a non-profit business?

- Do I want a sole proprietorship or an S corporation? (There are also other forms of ownership)

- Do I need to copyright or trademark anything?

- Do I have a business name?

Next is the big question, "where will the money come from?" A business plan can help to identify financial needs and goal setting. Contact the Small Business Development Center (SBDC) in your community and the Small Business Administration.

A word of caution – many businesses fail. You must have a passion for your idea, a good plan, and a willingness to put in long hours. It's exciting to see your idea become a reality, but it doesn't happen without a lot of hard work and commitment. (Excerpt from Women's Independent Press, September 2004)

Mary Murray is an attorney who has been in business for eight years. She is a sole-practioner in her law firm where she focuses on estate planning and administration.

Mary says that when she worked for her first law firm she enjoyed meeting people and assisting them with their wills and with estate planning. She decided then that this was the area in which she wanted to work.

Her most help came from a mentor that she can call with questions. When anything arises that is new to her he can walk her through it.

She found that it was important for her to watch what type of cases she took.

Her advice to women just starting out: Develop a business plan, determine when you want to work, and make your schedule flexible enough to include time for yourself.

Betty Murray has been a real estate agent for 15 years. She decided on this career because she felt it would be an extra income and, in addition, she could set her own work time.

Betty initially received the most help from a friend who took Betty under her wing and explained what was needed to be an agent. The most difficult problem she had was learning how to obtain customers and referrals.

She wishes she had known before starting the cost of being a part of the real estate field such as various fees that are charged and the cost of yearly education.

Her advice to women just starting out: Check all information before you go ahead. Find out all you can about fees, annual charges, company fees, etc.

Kathleen Yonker is a Nationally Certified Massage Therapist who has been in business for 10 years. She got into the business because of some work that was done on her making her realize how much relief can be attained from massage. Kathleen says that Business Networking International (BNI) has been her greatest marketing tool and support group. Her biggest problem in the beginning was to get through all the negativity she encountered.

Her advice to women just starting out: If you want it, go after it with everything you have. Just do it and doors will open for you. Know what you want, be specific, know your business inside and out. Be prepared to BE THE BEST- THEN TURN IT UP A NOTCH! Expect to do well and do not listen to those around you who are trying to talk you out of what you are doing. Never –ever stop learning about your business. Always be willing to give more than you receive. It seems like an oxymoron, but you will have the reputation for being the best.

H. David Holzer of Holzer Financial LP, Insurance Advisors has been in business for 48 years. David said he was working for a large company when the opportunity to have his own agency presented itself. He opened the agency with his wife taking care of the office duties. After he was in business for approximately 10 years his son decided he would like to work in the business as well. It's been a family business ever since.

His biggest help in getting started was the head stock broker for Moore, Leonard & Lynch who was a personal friend. When the children of his friend's clients were old enough to make their own decisions they would come to him to purchase investments. He would tell them, "You have to have a sound base first. After you buy your insurance come back to me." He would then send them to David. David said, "He was great!"

The biggest obstacle was finding clients to work with. David said that through different sources and his own searching it all worked out, "with a lot of hard work and long hours."

David wishes that initially he would have realized how much he enjoyed helping people to make the right decisions based on their wants and desires. He said, "I did that in the beginning of my business, but at that time I did more directing than listening."

His advice to women just starting out: Make sure you choose a profession you like. "When I first started in my profession I would talk to single people and young families and my biggest surprise was listening to what they would say about their jobs. They hated what they were doing. They would dread going to work on a Monday morning – I can't wait for Monday to come." He said, "Find a job you love, love the job and make it a part of your life."

Weston Lyon is the author of 10 books and is a Passionate Professional Speaker. For the past 9 years he has been in the business of Information Marketing. Weston says he is unemployee-able and started his first business while still in college. He actually dropped out of college prior to his senior year because he found that he liked business better and he also saw a bigger income potential than working for someone else. It wasn't only the money that influenced his decision, but also the fact that he could live in a style he preferred by being his own boss.

When he was starting his business he received the most help from an organization called BNI. Through this organization he was forced to re-evaluate his business, his marketing, and his communication style. He was also forced to go outside his comfort zone, while making money and meeting what has now become his "network."

His advice to women just starting out is to focus on your market more than on what you do. Find a market in people who will want what you have ...and pay for it.

Patti Harding is the owner of Muetzel Florist & Gift Shoppe. The business was established in 1947, but Patti has been the owner since 1999.

Patti said she has such a passion for floral arranging and for making people smile, and this business satisfies both. She said her husband found an ad in the newspaper saying that the business was for sale and he said, "Here honey, this if for you...go get it!" So she did with his 100% support.

Patti credits her past experience as being the most helpful to her when she began her business. She had been a supervisor of 7 women and that position made her tough, fair and self-confident. It also made her smarter and wiser through trial and error. This provided her with a great growing experience from the age of 19 to 36.

Patti says she had to learn to be patient and to be positive 98% of the time.

Her advice to women just starting out is to dream it and achieve it. Take tiny steps until you reach the top of the stairs. It won't happen overnight, but it *will* happen. Have a great spouse and/or friend to lean on and support you. BE POSITIVE no matter what happens.

Sam and Mary McMillen started Sam & Mary's Woodworks 32 years ago. They do furniture restoration, refinishing, and repair. Sam returned to Pennsylvania in December of 1976 after serving for 4 years in the U.S. Navy as a Navy musician. The economy was a mess and jobs were at a premium. He had a bachelor's degree in music education, but it was difficult to get a job in that field and he didn't particularly want to teach anyway. His degree made it even harder to get a job because potential employers felt that he would leave as soon as a teaching position opened up.

Sam and Mary married while he was in the navy and money was tight. In order to furnish their home they would buy "junk" furniture and repair and refinish it, learning as they went. It was a natural transition to open a furniture shop. Sam says that somehow, he always inherently knew how to do the work. What he didn't know, he read about or asked someone. He said it was a classic example of using their resources wherever they might be.

A real estate agent helped them to find their first shop. An attorney helped them to register their business, and an accountant helped them to understand the taxes and payroll issues. Sam says that these three are key to success along with proper and affordable insurance. He said strong and reliable agents are an absolute must.

Major obstacles included customer skills, work flow, employee management, and sources of supplies. They still require ongoing attention. Sam said, "After 32 years we still work diligently on improving our marketing and advertising skills. We have wasted a lot of money on ads that didn't work, didn't reach the right demographic audience or were simply way too expensive."

His advice to someone just starting out: Talk to another in a similar business. Set goals, and ask questions about every aspect of your venture. Know the costs before you hang out the sign and be prepared to eat, sleep, and breathe your business. Be prepared for long hours, multitasking a dozen problems at once, and every unexpected problem or behavior issue you can possibly imagine, and then some.

Mary Lee Gannon has been in business for 10 years. She is the author of the book *Starting Over – 25 Rules When You've Bottomed Out"*, she is a Cultural Turnaround and Leadership Consultant. Mary Lee is the owner of Gannon Enterprises – Complete Communications Solutions in a One Stop Shop.

Mary Lee is living proof that leading from a perspective of well defined values and strategies can turn a company or one's personal life around no matter what the odds.

At the age of 35 Mary Lee was a stay-at-home mother with four children under the age of seven. She was living the façade of a country club life while her marriage was crumbling. After filing for divorce she found that she and her children had gone from a lovely residential suburb to being homeless, without a car, hungry, and on welfare. She understood that she had to be the one to provide for her children and she had to decide how she could do that. Public assistance was not the way she wanted to live her life. She had an allied health degree but knew she could not make enough money with that to take care of her children.

Mary Lee created a life plan around the things she loved and in which she excelled. She identified her strengths and weaknesses. She developed her transferable skills and her sales skills to go on to become the executive director of a trade association where she also pursued and earned the designation of Certified Association Executive. This was her stepping stone to becoming a self-employed public relations consultant, journalist and business writer, all work she did from home while her children were young. Because she needed adequate health benefits for herself and for her children she decided to enter the corporate world. She taught herself how to network, fundraise and negotiate. She ultimately went on to be the President and CEO of a large hospital foundation and a national speaker. This was a far cry from living on welfare.

Mary Lee feels that her inquisitiveness was most helpful to her when she was starting out. She said she was fearless while not being reckless, and she asked questions or she figured out the answers to problems.

Mary Lee says the major problems she encountered were very little time to become successful because her children were hungry. She said, "I didn't have time to return to school, and I needed to learn things that would carry me far."

She wishes she had known that she should have abandoned all fear and set a five and ten year plan.

Her advice to women just starting out: Be fearless, not reckless and ask questions or figure it out.

Some quotes to help you along the way

There are times when we feel discouraged, and it is in times such as these that a quote can make the difference in our attitude for the day. The quotes below are encouraging and if you choose one that applies to you, and repeat it often, you will find yourself uplifted and ready to face any challenges that come your way.

The only real limitation on your abilities is the level of your desire. If you want something badly enough there are no limits on what you can achieve

There are only two options regarding commitment, you're either in or you're out, there is no such thing as life in between.

Only those people who will risk going too far can possibly find out how far one can go.

You can't communicate effectively unless people trust you. How do you gain trust? That's easy – be trustworthy.

We all need a little coaching. When you're playing the game it's hard to think of everything.

Every day do something that will inch you closer to a better tomorrow.

Excellence is not a destination. It is a continuous journey that never ends.

Dream big dreams. Only big dreams have the power to move your mind and spirit.

In the book of life's questions the answers are not in the back. (Charles Schultz)

Success is about making a difference – not just about making money.

Praise every improvement – even the smallest ones. Fill your mind with thoughts of peace, courage, health and hope. (Dale Carnegie)

Remember that unjust criticism is often a disguised compliment. (Dale Carnegie)

Analyze your own mistakes and criticize yourself. (Dale Carnegie)

A word, a thought, a new idea, a new perspective can change a lifetime.

Your consistent thoughts and actions become your reality.

For perfectionists, preparation often becomes procrastination.

Maintain a positive attitude. Every problem is an opportunity. Expect success.

Attitude is to life as location is to real estate.

Planning produces profits. Establish goals, priorities, and deadlines.

Do what you do best and delegate the rest.

He who believes succeeds. He who doubts fails. Sell yourself first.

The primary purpose of communication is to effect change. Keep it simple and sincere.

You have already done what it takes to be successful. Just to it more often.

Persist! Failing is not failure unless you fail to try again.

"That man is a success who has laughed often and loved much; who has filled his niche and loved his task; who leaves the world better than he found it; who looked for the best in others and gave the best he had." - Robert Louis Stevenson

"It is what you learn after you know it all that counts." - John Wooden

"People are always blaming their circumstances for what they are. I don't believe in circumstances. The people who get on in this world are the people who get up and look for the circumstances they want, and if they can't find them make them." - George Bernard Shaw

"Our greatest glory is not in never failing, but in rising every time we fall." - Thomas Carlisle

"The toughest thing about success is that you've got to keep on being a success." - Irving Berlin

"The quality of a person's life is in direct proportion to their commitment to excellence, regardless of their chosen field of endeavor." – Vince Lombardi

"If you have no critics, you likely have no successes." – Malcolm Forbes

"Success comes from listening. I've never learned anything from talking." – Lou Holtz

"Good humor makes all things tolerable." – Henry Ward Beecher

"Nothing is often a good thing to do, and always a good thing to say." – Will Durant

"If there is any one 'secret' of effectiveness, it is concentration. Effective executives do first things first, and they do one thing at a time." – Peter Drucker

"People who don't take risks generally make about two big mistakes a year. People who do take risks generally make about two big mistakes a year." – Peter Drucker

"Nothing in the world can take the place of persistence. Talent will not; nothing is more common than unsuccessful men with talent. Genius will not; unrewarded genius is almost a proverb. Education will not; the world is full of educated derelicts. Persistence and determination alone are omnipotent! - Calvin Coolidge

"Business is really more agreeable than pleasure; it interests the whole mind, the aggregate nature of man more continuously, and more deeply. But it does not look as if it did. – Walter Bagehot

"He that leaveth nothing to chance will do few things ill, but he will do very few things. – Charles Baudelaire

"You will never stub your toe standing still. The faster you go, the more chance there is of stubbing your toe, but the more chance of getting somewhere". – Charles F. Kettering

"Perseverance and tact are the two great qualities most valuable for all men who would mount, but especially for those who have to step out of the crowd." – Benjamin Disraeli

"No man can fight his way to the top and stay at the top without exercising the fullest measure of grit, courage, determination, resolution. Every man who gets anywhere does so because he has first firmly resolved to progress in the world and then has enough sitck-to-it-tiveness to transform his resolution into reality. Without resolution, no man can win any worthwhile place among his fellow men." – B.C.Forbes

"One's life work, I have learned, grows with the working and living. Do it as if your life depended on it, and first thing you know you'll have made a life out of it. A good life, too." – Theresa Helburn

Summary

The advice given by the successful people above covers almost any situation. If you read their words carefully you will find excellent suggestions that can be applied to your business efforts. By blending the wisdom they have learned and are willing to share with you and the advice given in the previous chapters you will have the advantage of avoiding many of the mistakes that can frustrate you and even cause you to give up your dream.

Chapter Thirteen

Lend a Helping Hand

Remember the help you received when you were starting your enterprise, or think about the frustrations you experienced and the times when you wished you could ask an experienced person for answers to your questions. Now it is your time to help someone else by passing on the knowledge you have gained from your entrepreneurial experiences. You will be amazed at the joy and satisfaction you receive when you extend a hand to a fledgling business owner. Just being there with a smile and a positive attitude can work wonders for the morale of a frightened and unsure future business woman.

Being available is one way to lend that helping hand, but there are other ways that are effective and appreciated.

Become a member of a mentoring program in your area. Many schools sponsor such programs as well as trade organizations. For instance, if your expertise lies in the field of accounting and you belong to an organization of accountants they probably have a mentoring program in place. Through this program you will be paired with an aspiring accountant and will be responsible for answering her questions and guiding her along the path to a business of her own. Schools also have mentoring programs. Let's say you are a beautician with a well established, profitable shop of your own. A local school for teaching and training beauticians would welcome you and be thrilled to have you take one of the students under your wing to advise her and also to give her a true picture of what is involved in owning a beauty salon. Mentors have become valued friends to the women they have helped to become established.

By this time you have been through the process of starting a business. It would be wonderful to share what you have learned and the perfect forum for sharing your experience would be as a teacher in your local community college. Community colleges offer a wide variety of subjects and would be able to schedule a class time that would fit into your schedule. This could be considered a form of mentoring, but it would involve a number of women instead of a personal one-on-one relationship. The plus side of teaching a business course is that you will be reaching several women and spreading your advice over a much wider field. With a one-on-one situation you will give help over a period of a year to only one person, with a teaching program you will be able to help 15, 20, or more women over that same period of time. And an added incentive is that you will also benefit in a monetary way because you will be paid to teach the class. It would be well worth your time to look into a local community college to see what arrangements can be made that would be beneficial to you, to the school, and to future business women.

As an active, successful business woman you should belong to at least one organization whose members consist of women entrepreneurs. It is at these meetings that ideas are exchanged and you have the opportunity to meet other women who will support you along the way. When you meet a woman who is trying to get started see to it that she attends meetings. She may be shy at first, thinking that as someone new to business she doesn't belong, but this is where your helping hand comes into play. Convince her that she will be welcomed and will gain knowledge by joining the group. If she is still hesitant, offer to pick her up and take her with you. If she can walk into the room with a friend she won't be nearly as frightened. You should introduce her and stay by her side for a short time, then start to back away a little so she will have a chance to mingle on her own, and in this way she will gain confidence.

When operating a business there are certain people that are necessary to you, such as an accountant, banker, and an attorney. If a person has no experience dealing with people in these professions it can be a daunting and intimidating task. They need to know they are choosing the right people to work with; people they can trust. You can provide an invaluable service for them by introducing them to professionals you know from personal experience to be honest and trustworthy.

A good way to get your name before the public and to interact with other women in business is to participate in trade shows. Here is where they, and their service or product, is viewed by the public. By encouraging a new entrepreneur to take part in a trade show you will be doing her a very big favor for which she will thank you in the future.

Summary

By taking the experience and knowledge you have gained and using it to lend a helping hand to others you will be performing a much needed service and you will feel wonderful about yourself.

There are many ways you can reach out to those who need your help. A few of these ways are:

Just be there for them.

Become part of a mentoring program

Teach a business class at a community college.

Take them to meetings where they will be in contact with other women in business.

Introduce them to people they will need to know for their business to run effectively.

Encourage them to participate in trade shows.

Chapter Fourteen

Enjoy Yourself

One of the reasons you went into business in the first place is because you were not satisfied with what you were doing previously and you found something that appealed to your sense of accomplishment and of pleasure. If those two ingredients are no longer a part of your life you will be no good to your business, your clients, or yourself.

If, in an effort to become successful, you have put so much time and energy into your business that you have neglected to factor in some "me time" you will soon become burned out and resentful. Don't wait for that to happen! Decide now, how many hours a week you will spend on yourself, then make sure to do exactly that. Keep in mind the old saying, "All work and no play makes Jill a dull girl." Another consideration is your health. Constant work and stress will be certain to take its toll on your health, so it's important to do what you can to prevent that from happening.

One of easiest and least expensive exercises is to simply walk. A walk of at least one half hour a day will do wonders for your health. If you like a more structured form of exercise a gym membership may be good for you. Here you will have the advantage of equipment and the company of others who are doing the same thing. If you can afford it, and it more to your liking, a personal trainer might be the best choice for you. Whatever you decide, don't hesitate to get started on an exercise program.

As for your "me time," make a list of things you enjoy. Is an evening at the theater what makes you happy? Do you like to go to a quiet room and read for a few hours? How about regular visits to a spa? Would that get your vote? Maybe you like to spend time shopping, not necessarily buying, but shopping nonetheless. Whatever it is that you enjoy, it is very important for you to allow time to do that. You will be a happier, more satisfied person, and that will also contribute to your success.

Summary

It is vital for your peace of mind and for your health that you do not neglect your health and that you pursue an enjoyable activity on a regular basis. Decide on a form of exercise you would enjoy doing and begin a regular program now. Don't put it off to a later date. List your favorite form of relaxation and factor it into your time schedule. Don't consider this as something you can cancel. It is every bit as important as a business meeting because if you aren't relaxed and happy you won't be an asset to your business.

This book was written as a resource and guide for women who are considering entrepreneurship and also as an aid to those already in business. It is my hope that every woman who has that burning desire to create her own business can gain valuable information from this book and that they will become happy, healthy, successful business owners.